Males, Nails, Sample Sales

EVERYTHING A WOMAN MUST KNOW TO BE
SMARTER, SAVVIER, SANER SOONER

Stephanie Pierson

SIMON & SCHUSTER PAPERBACKS
New York London Toronto Sydney

SIMON & SCHUSTER PAPERBACKS
Rockefeller Center
1230 Avenue of the Americas
New York, NY 10020

SIMON & SCHUSTER PAPERBACKS and colophon are registered trademarks
of Simon & Schuster, Inc.

For information regarding special discounts for bulk purchases,
please contact Simon & Schuster Special Sales at 1-800-456-6798
or business@simonandschuster.com.

Designed by Davina Mock

Chapter openers designed by Happy Menocal

Manufactured in the United States of America

1   3   5   7   9   10   8   6   4   2

Library of Congress Cataloging-in-Publication Data
Pierson, Stephanie.
Males, nails, sample sales : everything a woman must know to be smarter,
savvier, saner sooner / Stephanie Pierson.
p.   cm.
Includes bibliographical references.
1. Women—Life skills guides. I. Title.
HQ1221 .P54 2006
646.70082—dc22
2006045067

ISBN-13: 978-0-7432-6422-8

To Phoebe and Megan and Ollie.
All my children.

Contents

Contents

INTRODUCTION

Samuel Butler once said, "Life is like playing a violin solo in public and learning the instrument as one goes on." I say, *why*? Why practice hour after hour? Why practice *at all*? With me as your Suzuki teacher, you'll be a virtuoso right out of the box. I've lived it, done it, made all the mistakes, learned the ropes, and finally got it all down. Now I'll take you on a wise, witty whirlwind tour of everything *you* need to know: life skills, life lessons, and operating instructions; from the practical and the profound to the "who knew?"

Once you read this book you can expect a juicier chicken and a less hostile hairdresser. A better price from a wedding caterer. A name for your goldfish that you won't live to regret. A teenage daughter who won't even *think* of blaming you for her thighs, and a dog who will know not to jump directly on your breasts at night during a thunderstorm.

You'll know the right way to walk into a cocktail party; how to get a raise without crying; and how to break up with your shrink. In short, I'll teach you all the skills every woman needs for a more joyful life and a more rewarding lifestyle. Words like *regret, failure,* and *utter humiliation* will not be part of your vocabulary.

And lucky you. You won't have to marry a man and spend the best twenty-odd (I use the term advisedly) years of your life learning how to win arguments and get in the last word—I've done it for you. Thanks to me, *your* dog won't have what Dr. Bob, the $100-an-hour personal canine trainer, referred to as a "troubled adolescence" or be diagnosed with Reluctant Leader syndrome. Your child won't insist that the only movie she wants you to rent (and watches over and over) is the one about the kid who divorces her parents. You won't know the heartbreak of mistaking the cilantro for the parsley, buying the wrong house, breaking into tears when you try to describe your USB port problem to the tech-support guy, shopping retail and wanting to kill yourself when your best friend gets it for 75 percent off a week later.

Read this book and you'll know when you're ready for plastic surgery; why some women stay in coach and some get upgraded; how to order the right dish in a country where no one speaks English; what's the one word every mother of the groom needs to know; how to ask your most important global shopping questions in French, Italian, Spanish, Chinese, and Hebrew.

The average woman is presented with thousands of choices a day. I mean, just look at the toothpaste aisle of a good-sized drugstore. There are currently 61,935,508 women in America today between the ages of twenty-five and fifty-five who are forced *every single day* of their busy, important lives to figure out how to pick everything from a ripe cantaloupe to a wallpaper, from a career to a color for their bank checks.

It isn't just the sheer *number* of decisions and choices that makes it all so stressful. It's that it's hard to find things that make sense. Sure, advanced quantum physics makes sense. The Renaissance makes sense. Global warming makes sense. But not being able to find a bathing suit in a department store in August because they're already showing down coats makes no sense. Being told that a massage is a luxury, not a necessity makes no sense. The fact that Dame Edna, one of the most intuitive women alive today, is a man makes no sense. The idea that we can send a man, a woman, a monkey to the moon and self-tanners still streak makes no sense. And what to make of *this*? This country is filled with scientists and we *still* don't know if it is ever safe to have our eyelashes professionally dyed. On a slightly deeper note, politics and war make no sense, except for cola wars.

This book makes sense. The more we know and the sooner we know it, the easier our lives will be. And aren't you ready to read a book that gives you the kind of guidance you *need*—not just about better abs and better relationships *blah blah blah*, but one that can tell you how to order when the special of the day at the Japanese restaurant reads "Boiled Rabbi." The bottom line is that this advice is going to be a lot more up your alley than those familiar, formulaic women's magazines with their "helpful" tips.

Let's face it: we're all too busy running our lives and running the world to want to read six cookbooks to figure out why the mayonnaise curdled. And we want answers that work everywhere. If you have three days in Rome, do you really want to spend two of them researching antique silver picture frames? Or do you want someone to guide you to the outdoor market that's not in a guidebook that's got the best prices and, most important, one-of-a-kind frames you won't find anywhere back home.

Why me? My life experience is *huge* and I've really paid attention to all the lessons I learned (I'm not a girl for nothing). While there are a *few* areas I don't feel qualified to advise women on—like Brazilian bikini wax techniques, what's an appropriate Christmas present for your Kabala guru, the merits of thongs, and ménage à trois morning-after etiquette—I feel pretty good about everything else.

The results of my lifelong life as a woman speak for themselves: I dated for over twenty years. I was married for over twenty years. I've been divorced for two. I have two daughters. I have two female cats and one female dog. I have more close women friends than just about anybody I know. I have been to spas and shrinks. I understand the importance of killer lingerie and flexible hamstrings. I know from experience why there is nothing really "natural" about natural childbirth (ironically, during labor my doctor was on drugs while I was drug-free).

I have been profound: I've written definitive works on teen body image issues, lima bean festivals, the history of ketchup, tinted moisturizers.

I have been shallow: I was in some store somewhere, shopping, during every single national disaster from JFK to the *Challenger,* except for the August 2003 East Coast power failure—then I was right in the middle of a private Pilates lesson. The scariest medical news I ever got, I got on my cell phone when I was just finishing a facial and about to start my manicure.

I have had a breadth of experience: I have lived in the city (bad supermarkets, good manicures) and in the suburbs (great supermarkets, lousy manicures).

I can relate to women's endless quest for perfection: it recently took me six months to find the perfect toilet kit. Debating bronzers with my friend Patti got so heated that we just had to agree to disagree and not talk about it. Ditto the subject of rain shoes with my friend Marsha.

And although my many, many years in the trenches of womanhood and the fact that I have been wearing pretty much nothing but black for thirty years have given me a somewhat sophisticated take on life, I'm refreshingly down to earth. I honestly think I can relate to *all* women, *all* their hopes and dreams and cellulite issues. Surely it's no coincidence that my favorite nail polish is called I'm Not Really a Waitress.

I promise you that this book will be a confidence booster, a trusted friend, a mentor, and a life guide. It will be the wise, supportive mother so few of us are lucky enough to have. (Parenthetically, a neighbor once asked my own mother what had changed the most about her life since she had had children. I remember listening intently as my mom pondered the question, then responded, "I couldn't afford to buy designer shoes.") I'll address all life issues (even ones you might not have known you had), questions, and quandaries. And share the wisdom only a smart, successful woman who's been around—and I mean that in the best possible sense—

could. In no time and with minimal effort, you will have the right answers at your perfectly manicured fingertips. Your life will be easier and less stressful. You'll sleep better at night. It will be a better world. Men will be happier too. I will earn out my advance and win the Nobel Prize.

ONE

Life on Planet Woman

There are certain immutable principles a woman can live by. It's reassuring to know that while life is full of changes, some things *always* hold true. For example: The sun will always rise in the East and set in the West. The brown bear will always hibernate in the winter. Leftover Thanksgiving turkey, stuffing, and cranberry sauce will always make your refrigerator a better place. Wearing so much fragrance that your taxi driver asks you what fragrance you're wearing will never be something to brag about. No matter what the invitation says ("party festive," for example), accessorizing your look with fruit—real or plastic—is not a good idea. Always going out (even if it's cloudy) with something that has an SPF in it is something you need to do every day.

And there are certain things that a smart woman knows to steer clear of. Period. When you go to the nail salon, *never* cut your cuticles—just ask for them to be pushed. Don't have anything cut when you're having a pedicure, either. Never let anyone see your passport photo except the customs agent. Never attempt to speak or dress like a character from a book or movie. You don't really look like Amélie and you don't normally speak like Bridget Jones.

And while we're at *not* saying things, don't start saying "cheerio" and "brilliant!" and "lorries" after you've been in England for a few days. Ditto for France: don't start saying "quel" this and "quelle" that and trying to make those Gallic shrugs and face scrunches to show your indifference or disdain with *le monde* or *la vie*—or sprinkle your conversation with foreign words like I just did.

Be suspicious of places with foreign names that are mangled. There's a chain of beauty salons in New York called Amour de Hair. If *they* can't get the name right, do I trust them with my color?

Speaking of language, don't automatically correct someone who mispronounces a word. My friend Marsha Dick uses a technique that works like a charm. According to Marsha, it's okay to immediately correct someone if they're foreign because then you're actually *helping* them. But what to do about a friend who pronounces a word wrong? You don't want to flag this mistake in front of others and humiliate them, but on the other hand, you don't want them to keep making a fool of themselves. Marsha's solution is to hold off, not correct them when they first say the word, but instead use the very same word correctly in a sentence a few minutes later, make sure they are listening, and assume they'll get it.

Don't say something is the *new* something. As in, "Croatia is the new Greece" or "Beige is the new black" or "Rhubarb is the new green apple" or "Fifty is the new forty" or "Ginger is the new echinacea" or "Low-sugar is the new low-carb."

At the risk of being the hideous English teacher you hated, don't say "past history." If it wasn't in the past, it wouldn't be history.

Planet Woman would be a better place if there was no social one-upmanship. As in, "Yes, I did see *The Producers* when Nathan Lane and Matthew Broderick were in it. Twice. Once in previews." Or, "I remember when you couldn't get foie gras this good outside of Le Périgord." Or, "Isn't it dreadful what they've done to Santa

Fe?" Or, "You should have seen the *Mona Lisa* when it wasn't behind glass. What a shame you won't ever be able to." In the same vein, whether the talk is about Thailand, a trendy restaurant, a TV show, or a new gourmet cheese shop, don't ever say, "You've never *been* there?" or "You haven't *seen* it?" with a look that smacks of incredulity and superiority. A great example of this comes from an unnamed source (JoAnn, my ex-mother-in-law, may she rest in peace) who was a privileged world traveler. One day, she was talking to the lovely young social worker who was attending to JoAnn's elderly mother in her small Alabama town. JoAnn had just returned from a monthlong trip to Nepal with a museum group. She regaled the social worker with tales of the festivals, the fabulous hotels, the twenty-course banquets complete with honeyed fruits coated with edible gold leaf, and then just turned to the social worker and said with a certain noblesse oblige, "Well, you just *have* to go!"

Don't make your child's name a joke. If you're not Greek, don't name your child Zeus. And watch out for names like Sage and Chastity that can backfire. And don't—even if she's the most charismatic, adorable child and you're a nascent stage mother—give your baby a diva name. My daughter Phoebe had a friend at camp named Allegra LaViola. I always wondered what her destiny would be.

I have personally been there, done that, and regretted this, so I can only strongly suggest that you don't sing karaoke or country and western songs in public when you're sober or sleep with your boss when you're drunk. I have learned never to say, "Oh, I know that joke" when someone is in the middle of telling it. And I no longer start a joke, then immediately interrupt myself to ask, "Have you heard this one?" And finally, even if you have a fortune, don't pay a fortune for something simple like a T-shirt or tank top. That's why God created the Gap and Old Navy and Petit Bateau.

And finally, we need to be realistic about how old we are. While one size fits all these days when it comes to music and movies and StairMasters and restaurants and cool places to travel to, there just are some things you can pull off better when you're younger rather than older. And vice versa. One pleasure reserved for the very young is drinking and dancing the night away and still managing to muster the energy to make it in the next morning at 9:00 a.m. and put in a full, productive day. Whereas an older, senior executive gets to stay out too late, wake up with a hangover, and just not come into the office until 10:00 and no one can say anything. Same thing at in restaurants: the young and adorable get a table because of being, well, young and adorable. A woman of stature and reputation always gets a table because of who she is. Life on Planet Woman is extremely terrific, but no one ever said that it had a level playing field.

THESE ARE NOT WORTHY OF US

- Blueberry bagels, blueberry muffins, blueberry doughnuts that aren't made with real blueberries

- Anything in your kitchen that is colored Harvest Gold or Avocado Green unless you are being consciously retro

- Investing in mass-produced "art"

- Dressing according to your monthly astrological fashion profile

- Scheduling your wedding on a holiday (A truly frightening invitation would combine Memorial Day with New Jersey. An exception might be Christmas in Maui or Easter in Venice.)

- Cell phones on airplanes (the one place technology mustn't ever go); cell phones in the stall of the ladies room

- Aphorisms and inspirational sayings on everything from T-shirts to organic energy bars (On my Sleepytime Tea box, it says: "We turn, not older with years, but newer with each day.—Emily Dickinson." Did Emily Dickinson *drink* Sleepytime? Is she *endorsing* it? And on my bottle of Teas' Tea, this "award-winning" haiku: "White horse in the field of daisies. Whiter still.")

- Drinking wine out of Styrofoam cups

- Extreme *anything*

WE ALWAYS DESERVE THE BEST

These don't have to be profound. While love and friendship are wonderful things, so are peonies and Pilates and Maria Callas and Kiehl's SPF 15 Lip Balm, hue #58B.

- Italian linen
- Roses named after empresses and opera singers
- Anything in season, from strawberries to hot chocolate to flip-flops
- Stretching every morning when you get out of bed
- Watching your baby sleep, no matter how old he or she is
- A dog, a cat, a fish, a bunny you love who loves you back
- Seeing as much of the world as you can; getting away from home; going someplace for the first time
- Forgetting what day it is when you're on vacation
- Giving a surprise party for someone who wants to be surprised
- How you feel when a French person tells you you pronounced something right
- The moment before you kiss someone for the first time
- Coming home
- Reading *The Velveteen Rabbit* or *Goodnight Moon* out loud, even if it's for the millionth time
- Buying jewelry with semiprecious stones like peridot and lapis lazuli and labradorite and carnelian and tourmaline, not just because they're beautiful but because they *sound* so exotic and sexy (and you won't see everyone wearing them)
- Crisp, fresh, white anything, anytime, from pillow shams to shirts to flowers
- Giving a present that's priceless. When Phoebe turned twenty-one, I gave her the gift of knowing she would never again have to be "material" for articles or books I was

writing. Ever since she was little she has been featured prominently in everything I've written. Well, at least she got two years off. (Sorry, Phoebe.)

- Things that end in *ini*. Bikini, martini, Bellini. And okay, it's an e not an *i*: linguine
- A piece of your jewelry from your mother or grandmother
- Being a grandmother or a godmother or the aunt of an "honorary niece." You get to love them and then you get to go home

OXYMORONS FOR SMART WOMEN

It just helps if you know that even though people will say these words or phrases together, they don't actually *go* together.

- Low-key wedding
- Amicable divorce
- Comfy stilettos
- Simple outpatient procedure
- Simple outpatient procedure where you might feel some slight discomfort
- Advil is all you need if you feel some slight discomfort
- Undrinkable martini
- Spacious middle seat
- Extra legroom in coach
- Gourmet trail mix
- Low-maintenance beauty routine
- Cooking wine
- Crisp microwaved french fries
- Reasonably priced lawyer

THINGS YOU SHOULD NEVER HAVE IN YOUR HOUSE

- Mirrors all over your bathroom
- An au pair from France or Rio who is under twenty-two and has lacier underwear than you do
- A coed teenage slumber party
- The after-prom party
- The kindergarten hamster during Christmas break
- Too-prominently displayed pictures of yourself with celebrities
- A magazine they sell at my health food store called *Living Without,* which might as well just be subtitled *You Think You're Depressed Now?*
- Pictures of, old notes, or saved emails from an ex you still miss
- Ice cream if you're not eating ice cream—even if it's a flavor you wouldn't eat if you *were* eating ice cream
- Any art or decorative piece you got as a present that you've always hated but felt obligated to display
- An extra bedroom and a mother or mother-in-law with time on her hands

TWO

Must-Haves, Must Do's, Must Knows,
Must Bes, Musn't Bother With
or Worry About

There is great relief at the trillion things you don't need to *be* or *do* or *aspire to* in order to be happy. This can cover a multitude of experiences, from realizing that you don't have to have *all* the answers to your kids' questions to realizing that you don't even have to *try* to look like the six-foot-tall seventeen-year-old model wearing lamé hot pants in *Vogue*. At work, it's realizing that you can be a great boss without doing all the work yourself and that, actually, really good bosses delegate. It's realizing that you don't need to stay at the office until 11:00 at night to prove that you are a hard worker. It's realizing that you can say, "Yes, I do mind you putting me on hold." It's knowing that people will have a great time at your house even if you didn't make the mayonnaise from scratch and the pork roast was a little dry. That if you don't have a big formal dining room table, your friends will actually sit in your living room balancing plates on their laps and having a perfectly good time.

There is also relief knowing that there are some things every woman does need to own or know at some point in her life. And you'll need them whether you're married or single, straight or gay, rich or poor, twenty or fifty, living in Barcelona or Buffalo. Six come to mind immediately: you will always be glad to have a strand of pearls (and they don't have to come from Tiffany), a white shirt, a friend who loves you, a savings account, the best leather handbag you can afford, shoes you adore that actually fit. So in more ways than one, you will know you are starting off on the right foot.

YOU MUST BE ABLE TO

- Trust your own instincts
- Do research: Don't go into any situation without sound advice
- Know what's going on in the world: Read newspapers and books. Watch the news on more than one channel. Get the news online. Get a world view.
- Handle your money: Spend less than you make. Understand what's being deducted from your paycheck. Know why you did or didn't get a tax refund.
- Save
- Walk into a room where you don't know anyone and manage to mingle without sweating to death or having a panic attack
- Be an active listener: Really pay attention to what someone is saying—you'll stop thinking about yourself so much and you'll be making a real and solid connection
- Drive in the snow or on ice, with confidence—and know when *not* to
- Pick up a daddy long legs and dispose of it on your own
- Give back: Have a favorite charity. Volunteer. Contribute. Mentor.
- Read a map: Ask for directions

- Apologize to a good friend for behaving badly. Forgive a
good friend for the same.

YOUR MUST HAVES

We all have things and places and moments and mantras that sustain and comfort us and make us happy—the things that get us through the day and remind us that life is worth living. That never fail to delight and satisfy.

It's good to remember what yours are. If you're not in the mood to be creative or you're just plain lazy, you can share this must-have list, which I have culled from friends.

- Chocolate
- Friends, especially friends we still have from kindergarten
- Exercise
- Chocolate
- Pretty underthings
- Talks with our moms
- Red toenails
- Recipes for foods we love and make over and over again and never get tired of
- Pictures of adorable us as babies
- The perfect pair of black pants and a white shirt
- Chocolate

NECESSITIES VS. LUXURIES

There is a great deal of confusion about what is a *necessity* and what is a *luxury*. Who knows whether this came about because of confused men who didn't get it or because of guilty women who felt they weren't deserving of it. Whatever. This needs to be cleared up right away. To set the record straight, here are some luxuries that are actually necessities. My own rule of thumb is that if a so-called luxury makes you feel happy/terrific/fabulous/indulged/reinvigo-rated, then it's really a necessity. (Note that there is a difference be-tween "luxury" and "absurdity." "Luxury" is a scrumptious down pillow. "Absurdity" is the hotel that offers you a "Pillow Menu.")

- Massages
- Taking a Thai cooking course in Thailand
- Sheets with a high thread count
- Manicures (you actually *think* better when you've just had one—there must be some scientific proof of this some-where)
- Fresh flowers that make your whole house smell good
- Freshly squeezed juice
- Diamond studs (whether they're from Costco, QVC, or Bulgari)
- Someone to help serve and clean up at a dinner party if you're having more than eight people
- A health club membership
- A financial advisor, whether it's from H&R Block or JPMorgan
- Spas
- Down pillows and the best mattress you can afford
- A garden—even a window box; fresh herbs
- Heated pools
- Cashmere anything

FLOWERS

Ammi Simon, the manager of Surroundings Flowers (www .surroundingsflowers.com), says everyone loves

- Hydrangeas
- Tulips, by themselves

- Roses, cut short and arranged tightly—the only way to go with roses
- Hyacinths
- Sweet Peas
- Gladiolas, cut short

STAY AWAY FROM

- Carnations (especially dyed ones)
- Baby's Breath—with roses. Together they say "old prom" and uninspired florist. If you must have something, which you shouldn't, go with Queen Anne's lace.

YOU DON'T HAVE TO REVEAL YOUR AGE, BUT YOU NEED TO ACT IT

In an "anything-goes-and-aren't-we-liberated" age where there are very few rules, sometimes I think there should be *more* rules, especially when it comes to what's age appropriate.

- No woman over twenty-one should wear maribou or froufrou in her hair, unless you're Betsey Johnson or Björk. The exception is a single gardenia with an evening dress.
- A woman over fifty (unless she has no arm waddle) shouldn't wear a strapless evening dress without something—a shawl, a jacket—covering her arms.
- A woman over forty (unless she's Elizabeth Hurley) shouldn't go for teeny bikini.
- Don't try to dress like your teenager. You're *supposed* to look different from a kid.
- If someone can tell from ten feet away what kind of underwear you are wearing, the outfit is too tight/too revealing.

- A woman over forty (unless she's Elizabeth Hurley) shouldn't reveal too much skin.
- Don't wear anything from the vast Hello Kitty empire unless you're under the age of ten.
- Sweaters with Santa and bells or Jack o' Lanterns are also great if you're under ten.

HOWEVER . . .

We're all different, but we all need the same things in our closets and house and life. The basics for every woman at every stage and age:

- One outfit that makes you feel fabulous
- A roomy toilet kit that you keep stocked with those little sample shampoos and travel-size toothpaste so you're all set to go
- Luggage. Something handsome and sturdy that will with-stand savage baggage handlers and that doesn't look like every other piece on the carousel. Meaning: don't get one that's rectangular, black, with a bright colored ribbon you tie on the handle. Mandarina Duck is terrific; so is Kipling; so is Swiss Army. The heaviest hitter is Tumi, which almost never goes on sale. Muji (www.muji.com) has a se-ries of handsome basic carry-ons that are incredibly rea-sonable.
- Candles. Big, tea, and/or votive. And everyone from Ikea to Global Table (www.globaltable.com) to Bath & Body Works to the Wisteria catalogue (www.wisteria.com) has wonderful small colored glass or silver holders for tea can-dles and votives. Just beware those heavily scented candles that smell like a B&B from hell.
- Wineglasses (again, anywhere from Ikea to Tiffany): There are rounder, balloon-shaped glasses for red wine (the large opening lets the wine breathe) and slimmer glasses for white wine. There are also all-purpose wineglasses that are

perfectly fine. Champagne flutes are nice but not really necessary.

- Family pictures. And family dog or cat pictures. Not everywhere, but all clustered together either on a wall or a table.

- A great trench coat. It should fit perfectly and be waterproof and good for three seasons. Burberry or Ralph Lauren are classic but expensive. J. Crew or Club Monaco or Target or H&M are stylish and reasonable alternatives.

- Collections of things you really love, whether it's Arts and Crafts pottery or ceramic frogs. Just make sure it looks beautiful together.

- Your children's artistic creations and all their best report cards. Save their acceptance letters to college or jobs too, if you're sentimental.

- A set of good knives and a sharpener. A serrated bread knife, a carving knife, an all-purpose knife, a cheese knife, and steak knives. You will never regret getting a brand name like Wüstof or Henkel.

- Good pots and pans. Looks count and quality matters. The pots and pans you cook in affect the food you cook. And the really good cookware will not only last forever, but some, like cast iron and copper, get better with age. You can find them at every price point whether you shop at Kmart or Williams Sonoma.

- A few glass vases of various sizes. It's really hard to tell the difference between the ones from Crate & Barrel and the ones from Tiffany. Antique or deco vases—from flea markets or antique stores—will make you and your flowers happy.

DON'T BOTHER WITH

- That $500 cappuccino machine. You probably won't use it more than a few times, and it takes up about the same amount of space on your kitchen counter as a Mini Cooper. Why do you think God made Starbucks? Don't bother buying tiny espresso cups you won't use or tiny espresso spoons that you'll lose.

- Ditto pasta machines that will be relegated to your kitchen pantry after you realize how long it takes to turn out sixteen perfect ravioli

- Complicated exercise equipment. Most home exercise bikes turn into the world's most expensive clothes hangers. And there is no home décor they look good with. Same for all the rest of the equipment and tapes you bought at 3:00 a.m. on QVC that promised miracle abs and a tighter butt.

- Any piece of art that looks like it could go on a motel wall

- Any collection of dolls or stuffed animals from your childhood bedroom

- Books like *Jesus for Dummies* or the inspirational tome *Bagel Thoughts*

THREE

"I Don't Have Children, I Date Them":
Love, Sex, Men, Marriage, Divorce

From a posting at www.breakupnews.com: "Estelle Stribling, 37, would like the world to know that, at the age of 46, Michael Harris' only ambition in life is strutting around calling himself Sweet Daddy Cornbread.

Moderator's Quick Tip: If a guy calls himself Sweet Daddy Cornbread, you probably shouldn't date him."

"The men in your life may come and go, but female friends are yours forever. Never ditch the girlfriend for the guy."

—My friend Barbara

Liam McEneaney on his reasons for pursuing romance in internet chat rooms: "I was tired of women rejecting me for the way I looked. I wanted them to reject me for who I really am."

Men: can't understand them, can't change them, can't predict them, can't read their minds, can't control them, can't live without them. They are impossible and inscrutable and wired in ways that a master electrician couldn't begin to figure out. I still wonder why, only two months after what *I* thought was a wonderful time together at the high school prom (I even have the picture to *prove* it), my date decided to join the priesthood. And when a guy said we'd be in touch, did that mean we *will* be in touch? That he'll *touch* me? That I'll never hear from him again? Not surprisingly, aside from tips on how to get shiny, healthy hair, there is no other area where a woman gets more advice, most of it useless. What would country and western music be without heartbreak and betrayal? Just a couple of songs about old dogs, strong whiskey, and pickup trucks.

Some of the best advice on relationships comes from therapists who have seen it all, women who have lived it all, hairdressers who have heard it all—their experiences and observations can help save you from sure heartbreak or serve as a shining positive example worth following. With the advice in this surprisingly succinct chapter, you won't need to call your six best friends or pay someone to figure out whether a man is worth dating; intuit his real feelings before he does; understand why you keep making the same disastrous choices; know when to ditch him; decode what he is saying; decide whether to accept his proposal; order the wedding cake; get a restraining order as soon as possible.

You will discover which relationships are satisfying and why. When done with taste and tact, even breakups can enrich your life. When I was in my twenties, I went out with a guy named Leon who worked in his father's successful dry goods business; they supplied big department stores with everything from linen comforters to cotton pillow shams. When I broke up with him, I got to tell all my girlfriends, "It's curtains for Leon." Which we all found very funny. Then there is the story of a twenty-two-year-old woman who sent out cards to announce her engagement. A few months later, her fiancé jilted her for a coworker in his law firm. While totally devastated, this young woman had the presence of mind to have new cards printed. On the front it read "Single." And inside, "Picked the wrong guy. Gave him the wrong finger."

DATING

There are winners out there and love in the air—but there are also plenty of cautionary stories about the guys you need to catch and release once you discover their issues with little things like trust, honesty, giving, boundaries, sexual orientation, terminal meanness. Beware the frat boys who are twenty-five going on twelve. The princes whose mothers promised them a kingdom. The self-absorbed guys who can't remember your name in bed. The masters of the universe who are married to their CrackBerries.

Some you just can't see coming. This is from a young woman who worked at a New York shoe store: "My coworker, Jane, was engaged to a man for eleven years. One day, a few days before they were scheduled to fly down to St. Thomas for the holidays, they went to their weekly therapy session. Fifteen minutes before the end of the session, Jane's fiancé stood up and presented her with a contract, saying that she would have to clear out her belongings in a day, after which she would get ten thousand dollars. Then he left, leaving both the woman and the therapist stunned." The ending: Jane's fiancé moved to another state. The therapist didn't charge her for the session. Jane got $10,000. Eleven years is too long to be engaged.

Some you can see coming. My friend Mara was dating Donald, a successful psychologist who came across as both sensitive and sincere. One day, through a chance conversation with a mutual friend, she discovered that Donald was committing insurance fraud. It turned out that the main and most lucrative part of Donald's practice were Chinese clients who only spoke Mandarin. Donald didn't speak a word of Chinese. Mara confronted him. "How can you help these people when you can't even understand what they're *saying*?" "Well," said Donald, "you can learn a lot from body language." Mara is no longer dating Donald.

Friends don't let friends stay clueless. A recent college graduate writes, "One of my roommates had a boyfriend who was in a creative writing class with many of the people in her group of friends. She started to get odd questions and looks from them and didn't realize what was wrong until a friend in the class gave her some of the stories her boyfriend had written. In them, a character much like him argued lovelessly with his girlfriend. The girlfriend was needy, insecure, irritating, and shallow but was recognizably a version of her. And in the stories, the boyfriend character was only with her out of a fear of being alone. The entire class had been privy to his true feelings, and she had had no idea."

A recent Vassar graduate told me: "Sophomore year a sweet but odd guy I worked with asked me out, and I thought, Why not? Although he never actually took me out, he showed up at my room every day for a week. I began to realize that this was getting very creepy, but nothing compared to the Friday night when I came home late to find his coat on my floor and his wallet and ID cards spread all over the room. He had come to see me, and though no one was there, sat alone in my room waiting for me all night, getting drunk enough to leave his stuff there. The next day, I told him this wasn't going to work, and he called me frigid."

HOW YOU CAN TELL RIGHT OFF THE BAT IF A GUY IS NOT A "KEEPER"

- He says "product" for the stuff he uses in his hair.
- He says that a woman in his office is a "women's libber."
- You spent five hours baking tiny heart-shaped Linzer tortes for him and he says, "They're a little sweet."
- He's cheap. Guys who won't spring for a cab won't be generous with their affections or their emotions.
- The IRS calls him at home to talk to him about back taxes.
- He's depressed and depressing. For example, you cheerfully ask him how he slept the night before and he answers with a gloomy, "I'll live." All the Prozac in the world won't help.
- He turns off the TV in the room when he's leaving but you're still there watching it.
- He calls his mother two or three times a day.
- He hates his mother and he has never resolved his issues with her.
- He doesn't use turn signals and honks incessantly when he's driving.
- He gives you nose clippers or a King Tut tissue holder box as a present.
- Mandals
- He tells you his idea of the perfect woman is his sister. And then when she visits, he flirts with her.
- He makes fun of you in front of his friends. He makes fun of your friends in front of you.
- All his gifts are completely generic, like red roses and teddy bears. If he doesn't know you well enough to think of some-

thing more personal than a teddy bear, you're in trouble. (This doesn't apply if you love teddy bears.)

- He himself loves and collects teddy bears.
- He says things like "I hate quotation marks." Huh?

Mandals

From a twenty-three-year-old woman who notices these things: "Oh, how I hate mandals. Let me explain. Feet can be beautiful, as anyone who's seen a tanned, smooth, well-taken-care-of foot can attest. However, feet can be ugly. And unfortunately it's a safe bet that most men's feet will fall into this second category. Which is why, come spring, suddenly it seems that hundreds of pasty, hairy, unkempt, gnarly man toes begin to appear, as often as not peeking out from a pair of old beaten up Birkenstocks or decrepit shower shoes. Now, I don't mean to be unfair—there are men who seem to have looked at their feet and cleaned them up accordingly knowing that other people, too, will have to look at them. And these men will probably be wearing a lovely pair of leather flip-flops, perhaps, and all will be well. However, these men are rare. And probably gay. So I will make a sweeping pronouncement—*Men: put your feet back in their shoes.*"

SIGNS OF A KEEPER

- He's still friendly with his exes. (I said *friendly,* not obsessed and/or still in love with.)
- He goes out for soy milk and comes back with flowers.
- He knows what your favorite animal, flower, and food are.
- His relatives meet you and say, "So you're the famous _____!"
- Your mom likes him.
- Your dog likes him.

- He loves the way you look in the morning.
- He lets you read in bed with the light on even though he wants to sleep.
- He knows that it's easier to send flowers than apologize, but he makes the phone call and skips the tulips.
- He carries your groceries and takes out your trash.
- He doesn't tell you that you talk to your mother too much.
- He lets you name the baby.

HOW DO YOU KNOW HE'S THE ONE?

"I just felt right at home with Ben. Comfortable from the get-go. That was simple."

—My recently married daughter Megan

"If he sees you as a separate person to be evaluated; he acknowledges your separateness; he brags to other people about the stuff about you that isn't obvious. It's a public acknowledgment. And he has to be emotionally *available*—not just present—he has to be available to invest in you."

—Marjorie Kalins, television production executive

"You know a guy is special when he's said something to you that's clicked—that makes you think—oh my God, he *gets* me."

—A journalist with a relationship that's ten years old and going strong

"If you're so attentive to the other person and imagining—If only I was a rose, not a geranium; left-handed, not right, it would all work out—that's when you need to realize it's *never* going to work. On the other hand, if you can be who you *really* are and he loves you for being a geranium . . ."

—A friend who has never lacked for worthy boyfriends

GENDER STUDIES, OR, WHY JUST BEING "GAY" IS PASSÉ

So you're okay with the term *gay*, and *lesbian* is a comfortable addition to your vocabulary. But these days there are (almost) as many terms as there are sexual variations. Here's a few to tuck into your speech patterns, thanks to Anika Chapin for her gender genius:

Metrosexual: also known as "fauxmosexuals," these are a species of primarily urban men (hence the "metro") who exhibit characteristics that are often associated with gay men. These are: a fastidious vanity and care for appearances; an interest in fashion and design; a willingness to spend great amounts of money on all of these. Soccer star David Beckham, who wears nail polish and occasionally skirts but is undeniably straight, is considered the poster boy of the metrosexual. The guy friend who confessed to being on the waitlist for the new Jack Spade messenger bag while also admitting to having a secret crush on Kate Spade is a metrosexual.

LUG/BUG: This is a specific phenomenon that tends to happen on college and high school campuses; young people take advantage of this time to experiment a little, and earn the title of LUG or BUG, "Lesbian Until Graduation" or "Bisexual Until Graduation." (Why there are no GUGs, I'm not sure.) Often the term has a negative connotation, indicating that someone is not really gay or bisexual, but just being trendy.

Hasbian: This is the term for a woman who once was a lesbian and now is in a heterosexual relationship. Anne Heche, who shot to fame as the girlfriend of comedian Ellen DeGeneres, only to leave her and settle down and procreate with a man, is the classic hasbian.

Pansexual (or "ambisexual"): Forget gaydar. The pansexual is that rare creature that sets off all alarms. Men? Sure. Women? Sure. Many at the same time? Of course. Barnyard animals? Why not. Shoes? Mannequins? Vegetables? Bring 'em on down. The pansexual is omnivorous, mysterious, and strangely attractive—think Alan Cumming.

Luppies: Generally young, upwardly mobile lesbians.

The Gayby Boom: The sudden proliferation of gay couples having or adopting children.

ROMANCE

From a twenty-four-year-old who has a boyfriend who is very lucky to have *her:* "A relationship, in my view, is between two very unique individuals, complex combinations of likes and dislikes and experiences. The *least* romantic date I ever had was at the top of the Empire State Building, right before it closed down, where my date and I looked out over the city and shared a kiss in the twinkling lights. All I could think was how I felt like I was in a movie, not my own life, and how the perfect setting couldn't hide the nagging sensation that the guy wasn't right for me.

"What I do like is the kind of romance that is completely unpredictable, because it is entirely born of the moment and the people. It could sneak up while burning popcorn, or playing Ping-Pong, or cleaning up after a dog. It could be a blurb in the newspaper read out loud, or watching the Naked Cowboy sing in Times Square. I would trade a thousand Empire State Building moments for the one when I lost my balance out of the blue and fell into the deep snow, and the guy I was with fell in next to me so that we could be twin Yetis, icy and freezing and klutzy. It isn't a scene that would ever be found in a novel with Fabio on the cover, but it was a moment of shared connection, ours alone, and that is forever romantic."

One of the major loves in *my* life was the writer who, after our first stupendous and magical evening together, said to me the next morning, "Before I met you, I was *living* but I wasn't *breathing.*" I know it sounds like a bad Lifetime movie line, but I was floored by the sheer poetry. Hmmm . . . maybe it *was* a bad Lifetime movie line.

WEDDING WISDOM

From the newlywed

"On your wedding day, don't lose sight of the reason you're doing it. It's not just the one day you're a fairy-tale princess with anxieties about whether you've got on too much eyeshadow and if your bouquet is too sparse—you're marrying the man you love."

—Megan Connell

"Think long and hard about whether you want an outdoor wedding. The weather was so iffy and even with a tent, we worried about wind and rain. And the week in June that we got married was unseasonably cold. Luckily, the skies cleared just in time."

—A bride who married at their upstate country house

Thank you's matter: I got a handwritten thank-you note inside a CD of the newlyweds' favorite music, some of which they played at the ceremony, with a great shot of the wedding tent on the cover.

You don't have to spend a fortune on a dress. From Liz Grossi Strianese, stylist and owner of Relic, a vintage store in Beacon, New York

"I'm a believer in thinking outside of the box. I had my wedding dress custom made and it only cost a few hundred bucks. I bought the silk in the fabric district and designed it myself. One could easily clip photos of what they like, if they can't draw. I would do this again with a good suit. Men have custom-made suits all the time, why not us?"

From the Mother of the Bride

"Be inclusive. Invite the groom's parents to everything: have them come to the tasting; to look at the possible locations. Reach out, share, consult." Also, "Ask yourself, What do you expect from the wedding? Are you putting on a show or are you having a party with your friends and family? How do you want the wedding to feel?"

—Carol Helms, a New York interior designer

"The hardest thing was the guest list. It gets out of hand no matter what. Talk about the number of guests early—you can't get the space until you know. Then, if you can, find a space that offers some flexibility with numbers so you're not stressed if 100 percent of the invitees accept."

—Marylin Silverman, a marketing consultant

From the Mother of the Groom

"As the mother of the groom you have no vote. Praise, praise, praise. As in "The shocking pink tablecloths look fabulous! All those little votive candles were a stroke of genius!" And if you simply can't *praise*, the word is *wow!* An ice sculpture of the bride and groom. Wow! She's coming in to the synagogue on a white horse? Wow! This same rule can be used later when the happy couple is about to have a baby. As in, "You're naming the baby Harpo? Wow!"

—Bobbi Schlesinger, a public relations executive

"The classic advice to the mother of the groom: 'Shut up and wear beige.' Now that she's the veteran of two weddings, my friend has concluded: 'shut up' is right. 'Beige' is wrong."

—A woman who has two married sons

Wedding Food

You can go simple, homey, and unpretentious—think fried chicken and deviled eggs—or you can go all the way to black-tie cater-waiter world and cracked crab en croute with tomato coulis. Just do your homework: interview caterers, taste all the food, sample all the wine, create a wedding cake that can be anything from traditional tiered to a tower of cupcakes. Do what two foodie friends of mine just did: knowing that they didn't want to be slaving over a hot grill during their reception, they found a chef who would faithfully follow their own sparerib recipe.

And food snobs be damned: one of the most sophisticated women I know had a chic, stylish evening wedding and decided that one of the hors d'oeuvres had to be the one she loved most: Pigs in a Blanket. And along with the caviar and blini and the Brie de Meaux, proudly displayed on antique silver trays were Pigs in a Blanket with ballpark mustard.

Of course, simple doesn't mean cheap. Food writer Jonathan Reynolds was shocked at how high the caterers' bids were on the upcoming wedding that he was planning. A friend said to him: "When caterers hear the word *wedding*, they start adding on the zeros." So Mr. Reynolds suggests: "You might want to tell them you're planning a wake and see what happens."

In-laws

It's amazing what a little space can do. As a general rule, don't live *with* or *close to* your in-laws. Once it comes to babysitting, rethink.

Pick your battles. "My mother-in-law is extremely traditional (not to mention controlling!) and she wanted certain things *her* way at our wedding. There was no negotiating with her—I didn't let it be a deal breaker between us."

—A preternaturally smart newlywed

"You have to give up the illusion that you're gaining another family. I think you're lucky if there are good feelings all around. But after all is said and done, it's just the group that comes along with the person you love. So you don't have to try to work impossibly hard at making it work."

—Writer and contributing *Newsweek* editor Dorothy Kalins

"If your mother-in-law cooks, ask for recipes even if you have no intention of making them."

—My friend Emily

Some in-law interactions are simply weird. My then-husband's aged grandmother lived in Alabama. During a pleasant family visit from him and our daughter Phoebe, then around six, the grandmother turned to Tom and, looking straight at Phoebe, whispered loudly, "Her momma *dead* yet?" Which seemed funny at the time.

From the Happily Married

My friend Helen told her shrink how sick and tired she was of arguing with her husband, Tim, because he never seemed to listen, even though it was clear to Helen that she had the most compelling points and made the most sense. Then she gave some examples that proved her point. The shrink looked at her and said, "Helen, it's very simple: you can be right or you can be married."

> "Acknowledge that you are two different people, that he is not supposed to be your soul mate (whatever that is) or to complete you (no one can do that—only you) and that shared values will take you a lot farther down the road than shared hobbies or favorite drinks."
>
> —A woman who got married at twenty-three and is still happily married twenty-five years later

The big problem with hyphenating your names when you get married is monogrammed towels. Say that Grace Yu marries Norm Schwartz and gives birth to Lily Rose Yu-Schwartz, who will someday marry Jason Hue and turn into Lily Rose Yu-Schwartz-Hue. As an aside, I've noticed that people with unusual names tend to marry people with unusual names. When I was growing up in Baltimore, Dootsie Duer married Snuffy Leach. Last weekend I spent time with a middle-aged couple named Ginna and Jimmer.

> "Be realistic. What you see is what you get. 'I love you, you're perfect, now change' is how many people get married. Your partner is not perfect—accept it. Nor are you."
>
> —Alexis Johnson, a Westchester, New York, psychotherapist who does a lot of couples therapy

To achieve a good, strong marriage, Dr. Johnson notes that "good sex is very helpful." (Well, that's a fun one to work on.) And she offers a few things worth thinking about:

1. Relationships work because you are on the path to self-enlightenment. You can't expect your partner to make things work.

2. Teamwork and common goals are important.

3. Direct communication is essential—don't badmouth your spouse.

4. Examine whether the giving and taking in your relationship is balanced.

BREAKUPS

From my friend Liz who left both her boyfriend and Seattle: "Don't move to a strange city to be with a man." I would add, "Don't move to a familiar city with a strange man."

Next to wedding announcements, websites that post recent breakups are impossible not to read, and—unlike the wedding announcement of some gorgeous young couple with bright prospects and rich families—these breakup stories and announcements don't leave you with a case of "Why couldn't it be me?" Who doesn't want to hear the juicy details of love gone *really* wrong? Like this announcement from twenty-nine-year-old screenwriter Flint Wainess's www.breakupnews.com titled: "Cohen/Pomarolli." It reads, "Kerri Pomarolli, 25, a Los Angeles comedienne, and Joshua Cohen, 30, a New York businessman, recently ended their bicoastal relationship due to irreconcilable religious differences. Pomarolli was devastated by the breakup, but said there can be 'only one j.c. in my life.' She also said it's nice to be able to eat pork again without feeling guilty."

DIVORCE

Why do they say "her marriage *collapsed*" or "*broke down*" or "*fell apart*"? It sounds like what happens to a building built without adhering to code. Even worse, "her marriage *died*." The safest thing to say is "her marriage ended in divorce."

Coincidentally, the *buzzwords* of divorce are also the biggest *oxymorons* and *lies*. There's not a letter from counsel to counsel that doesn't say "hoping we can settle this *amicably*" or "looking forward to a *fair* settlement" and is always signed—by the attorneys and the spouses—"*respectfully.*"

When a couple goes through a divorce proceeding, they find themselves saying (and hearing) phrases and lines that they never in their whole lives thought they would be saying. Divorce is a Jerry Springer world. Phrases like "Get out of my house and my life!" and "You're a scheming, conniving, lying son of a bitch" are just par for the course.

One of the most common questions when a couple gets divorced is whether you can stay friends with both. A friend who is open and nonjudgmental says: "No. You can be friendly and cordial toward both, but in the end, your loyalties have to go one way or the other. It's usually an easy choice, since you were his or her friend or colleague first, in most cases."

How to keep your dog in a custody battle.

From divorce lawyer Raoul Felder: "Start a diary showing that you are the primary caretaker. Note how many times you walk the dog."

Finding the right divorce lawyer is like finding anything: do your homework to make sure this is a person who is well known and well respected in the field. Make sure you can comfortably relate to him or her because you'll be revealing some of the most intimate details of your marriage (and I mean *intimate*). As best you can, find someone who will really listen and tune in to what is most important to you, whether it's custody or maintenance or just a quick and painless resolution. And talk fast: these lawyers practically charge by the breath at a time when you really want to talk. A good marriage is priceless. A bad divorce is expensive.

It's not just what you've decided to do and who represents you—it's *when*. Karen Rosenthal, a top New York divorce lawyer and partner in the firm of Bender Burrows & Rosenthal, says, "Time to wait is a big help." She advises her clients not to rush into a proceeding. "If you can wait until you calm down, you can deal with everything less emotionally, you'll be less reactive." She adds that "even with some waiting, a woman who is emotionally damaged and reactive doesn't want to give anything, especially if she's the breadwinner." In Ms. Rosenthal's experience women in our culture are not raised to be the primary providers for the family financially. "It's hard to make my clients understand the law regarding equitable distribution. What they tend to feel is that what the law *says* is right doesn't take into consideration what's fair or right given the facts of *their* marriage and the type of contributions made. That is where the lawyer's zealous representation comes in."

So, time does allow for both parties to cool off. A free tip from Ms. Rosenthal: "Here's another truth about time that works in the opposite direction. If a party has cheated in the marriage and a generous offer is given soon after the other spouse finds out about the affair, grab the deal—it's a guilt offering and will only go down from there." She adds that this onetime offer comes from the breadwinner—male or female—who wants to get out quickly and will pay a high price for exiting.

At her huge and lovely wedding at one of Boston's most celebrated churches, my friend Belinda had both her parents and Sam's parents walk down the aisle with them. After the vows, a beaming Belinda and a radiant Sam kissed. Then Belinda kissed her dad. Then Sam kissed his mother—in one of the longest, most passionate, most inappropriate kisses since Angelina Jolie kissed her brother at the Academy Awards. Mouths dropped open. We were all (including Belinda) transfixed. Belinda got very, very drunk at the reception. Within a year, Belinda and Sam had divorced.

From my friend, Dr. Harriet Blumencranz, a retired pediatrician: "I, myself, had *two* nonamicable divorces and there were no kids. In my whole twenty-five years of pediatric practice, I saw maybe two divorces that didn't result in anger and recrimination. And in those cases, the exes quickly and happily remarried more suitable mates."

Finally, if you think you're going to separate from your husband, don't buy the giant economy size of anything.

Even if he done you wrong, the courts don't care. The divorce laws in every state are different, but you don't automatically get more sympathy or money because he behaved badly.

The easiest thing to say when someone asks you why you got divorced is "incompatibility." The easiest thing to say when someone asks you how you are doing, no matter how you're doing, is "I'm moving on." Moving on is easier when you are like my divorced friend Karen. When asked about her marital status, she simply says her husband is dead. Another friend who is "moving on" reads the obits every day looking for her ex-husband's name.

My friend Betsy just got divorced and due to her husband's business failures, she is now living alone on a greatly reduced scale. So when her college roommate—newly divorced from a partner at a successful investment firm—told Betsy that she should just "let go of the anger," Betsy pointed out that it is a lot easier to let go of anger when you are holding on to a large apartment, a ski house, and a hefty cash settlement.

A great divorce line that kind of sums it all up: Two of my friends were discussing the first one's terrible divorce. The first recited the litany of her divorce: "He lied. He cheated. He acted like it wasn't his fault. He wouldn't even give me a decent settlement." Her friend sighed and said, "What's not to hate?"

MEN ARE FROM . . .

Women's brains are wired differently than men's. My friend Mark Finley tells of having a conversation riding in the car with his mother; they talked about a lot of things during an hour-long trip. In the middle of a discussion about college applications, Mark's mother said, "No, I don't really think it's worth getting it rewired after all." Mark said, "*What* are you talking about?" "Well," his mother said, as if it were perfectly obvious, "the dining room *chandelier*." "But we talked about that when we first got *into* the car," Mark said. "How am I supposed to know you've gone back to the dining room chandelier?" "Well, your sisters would all track it *perfectly*," his mother answered.

FIVE ESSENTIAL TRUTHS ABOUT MEN

- "With men, *subtle* doesn't work," suggests a friend of mine who is on her third (happy) marriage.

- Men think they're better drivers than we are.

- A man will never understand why a woman can never have too many black sweaters.

- Men have been conditioned to believe that the flowers women love the most are long-stemmed red roses. And many believe that the roses from the corner deli (the ones that never *open* and have no smell) are just what women look for in a flower. Who would have the heart to tell them we'd rather have French lilacs?

- "You don't really know a man until you hand him the remote."—Victoria Roberts, *New Yorker* cartoonist

FOUR

Great Kids, Happy Families, and Only Flushable Pets

"If a woman has to choose between catching a fly ball and saving an infant's life, she will choose to save the infant's life without even considering if there are men on base."

—Dave Barry

"If your kids can't count on *you* to humiliate them in public, who can they count on?"

—Barbara Harrison, creative consultant

"Before I was married, I had three theories about raising children. Now I have three children and no theories."

—John Wilmot, Earl of Rochester, 1647–1680

My sister-in-law Abigail's four-year-old son, Alexander, looking at Abigail as she changed her clothes: "Mommy, did you grow some pounds?"

Families—both the one you grew up in and the one you start—call to mind the same simple aphorism: *Raise your hopes and lower your expectations*, which I *think* is original, but perhaps I have mistakenly stolen it from a needlepoint pillow, a Woody Allen movie, or the captain of a British warship.

Lowering expectations: there's actually not much you can do about the family you were born into since it's way too late to pull off that "I must have been adopted" excuse. *Raising hopes:* this chapter will share the joys of raising your own fabulous family and help answer any questions that might be standing between you and true maternal bliss.

All mothers have questions, especially *new* mothers. Like "Didn't I used to have a sex life and a life and a mind and a flat stomach? And when do I get all that back?" Mothers of very young children have questions. My friend Leigh was crestfallen and confused when her daughter Lindsay's first word turned out to be "money." When their children are slightly older, mothers have more questions. Like, why do kids never lose *two* of anything? And why do kids with dirty hands only put them on *light* surfaces? Mothers of teenagers (especially teenage daughters) want to know where to go for tattoo removal, how long peroxide lasts in hair, and what terrible thing they did in a former life to deserve this.

What makes motherhood hard from the very beginning is that you are sleep deprived for months and I don't think you ever quite recover. It's like a lost weekend in Las Vegas, only there's projectile vomit all over your nightgown. And motherhood is so unquantifiable. It's not like work where you get raises and have an assistant who never cries when she's teething.

How do you really *know* how you are doing? There *are* actual moments when it becomes totally clear how you are doing. I gave birth to a child who was a physical Mini Me, yet when she was out on the street with her beloved Trinidadian nanny, Enid, and someone asked Phoebe who she looked like, she would look lovingly up from her stroller and coo, "Like Enid."

Another moment of truth was the day when Phoebe (age five) turned to me and said sweetly, "Mommy, I hate Daddy much more than I hate you." Of course, sometimes you do have to read between the lines a bit. When he was nine, my friend Dorothy's son asked her, "Mom, would you rather I run away or would you rather pay me for *not* running away?"

What I quickly realized is (a) how could they not ultimately love you when your heart's in the right place, and (b) that there are many different types of mothers, so you shouldn't worry if you seem to be handling situations differently from other mothers around you. It's not a competition (well, only to get into nursery school, elementary schools, any private school, all colleges, and of course graduate school, not to mention Little League and soccer and tennis teams, gymnastics, cheerleaders, plus the school play and the summer camp musical). And now it seems to be a competition as to who has the most expensive stroller ($800?!) and who has toilet trained her child earliest (six months?!).

The nice thing about getting to know other mothers is they often make you look sane by comparison. Once, when it was a snowy no-school day, I was sledding in the park with a bunch of mothers and kids from Phoebe's elementary school. "Doesn't your daughter want to go down the big hill? I'll take her," I said to one of the mothers. "Oh no. I can't risk that. She's a skater and she's training for the Olympics. What if she twisted her ankle?"

But mothers *are* different. A few years ago, I was on a talk show with Phoebe for the book I had co-authored about teenage body image issues. The topic was exactly that—different types of mothers. The host of the show asked Phoebe (age nineteen) what kind of mother I had been, and Phoebe—without missing a beat—answered, "Very anxious." I turned and shot Phoebe a look and she quickly amended, "But loving." She looked at me and added: "*Very* loving."

Due to the child-rearing practices I followed (a lovingly befuddled but well-meaning permissiveness; a well-meaning but misguided micromanagement), our dog Ollie turned out *exactly* the way Phoebe did, with the *exact* same character traits and personality, the only real difference being that we didn't have to send him to college. So at least I was consistent. Except for safety issues (don't even *think* of stepping into the street without looking both ways; the stove is *hot*!), neither Phoebe nor Ollie heard the word *no* from me until they were both well into adolescence, although we never really knew *when* Ollie went through adolescence since he seemed "troubled" for so long. We had to take Dr. Bob, his remedial trainer's, word. Megan, my oldest stepdaughter, got a fighting chance for excellent mental health, since she lived most of the year with her nice, sane mother, Katherine, in Berkeley, California.

My mother—who, when a college boyfriend of mine asked what color my hair had been in childhood, replied "mousy brown"—was just a *little* less overwhelming than I could have hoped for in her maternal enthusiasm, so it is no surprise that I went in the opposite direction. There was nothing I wouldn't give, bestow, praise to let Phoebe and Ollie know how special they were to me. Which is probably how I got the toddler who asked for a glass of apple juice and then when you said "What's the magic *word*?" would reply *"Now!"* And which is probably why, when Ollie was five, he was diagnosed as having something called Reluctant Leader syndrome. RLS, a little-known canine syndrome, occurs when the dog is confused about who his leader is. When my then-husband, who was clearly the alpha male in the house, left for work, Ollie was left with me and Phoebe. Phoebe was like a sister so she and Ollie had a clear sibling relationship, but I was so inconsistent in my leadership or so perplexed that sometimes I was in charge and sometimes Ollie was. And sometimes, no one was. Ollie was confused about what his role was and so he acted out. His whole life was a troubled search-and-destroy mission.

What could I have done that would have been of use to me and Phoebe and Ollie? Some of this is so basic that I had to ask a friend who is a kindergarten teacher to help me anyway. Most of this pertains more to Phoebe than Ollie, since kindergarten teachers don't advise parents of collies.

1. I could have said no. And meant it. I should have never framed a sentence by leaving it open ended—e.g., "We're going to go to the park now, okay?" Skip the "Okay?"

2. I could have given them limited choices—"Do you want the shredded wheat or Cheerios?" "Do you want to wear the red or blue sweater?"—so they could *feel* empowered, even though *I* was in control.

3. I could have set boundaries. My friend Marcell Greenfield, who was voted the most well-adjusted woman in college, not only set boundaries for her three kids, she *acted* on what she had said *immediately* and *nonverbally*. "If I had already explained to one of my children that something was not acceptable and he or she was about to do it anyway, I would give a quick squeeze of his or her hand as a reminder. And that way, I didn't have to reprimand. It was so simple and clear."

4. I shouldn't have said yes, then no, then maybe, then yes, then landed on "Ask Daddy."

5. I could have explained that actions have consequences and made

sure I followed through instead of starting with "If you don't do . . ." then vaguely trailing off. Voice coach Laura Menard was explaining something she expected *her* young daughter, Isabel, to do and Isabel was being resistant. "I don't see *why* I have to do that!" They were in the car. "Well," said Laura, "what if I didn't want to stop at all these red lights and just drove straight through them?" "You can't *do* that!" Isabel said, horrified. Without being confrontational, Laura quickly made the point that there are rules to follow and consequences if you don't.

6. I should have been the grown-up. Or at least, in moments of indecision or impending crisis, *impersonated* one.

7. I shouldn't have given Ollie treats when he was bad just because I knew he didn't *mean* to be bad and I wanted him to like me.

8. I shouldn't have let Phoebe cheat at Candyland.

NEWBORNS

Joy mixes with anxiety. Both are sleep deprived. Babies don't know if it is day or night. Funny, neither do you.

"I used to put Lincoln right next to our bed at night and was worried every time he made a sound, then equally worried when I *didn't* hear a peep out of him. It took me a while to relax and trust that he would make it through the night."

—From my friend Dorothy

The good news: "By the time they're eighteen, they *won't* be sucking their thumbs, they *will* be toilet trained, and they *won't* be sleeping in your bed."

—Sydny Miner, publishing executive and mother of two capable sons

- "I can't do it all" is an excellent mantra. Start now.
- Never wake a sleeping baby.
- The single biggest reason most couples have a second child is because they're curious to see what the new one looks like.

55

- When they sleep, you sleep.
- Contrary to what you always hear, you never forget a *minute* of your childbirth experience.
- Get the epidural.
- A coworker told me that her sister had recently given birth to twins and that her sister now had what my colleague referred to as "postmortem depression." I *think* it was a slip of the tongue.

LITTLE KIDS AND MEDIUM-SIZE KIDS

- Kids are born knowing their Miranda rights. "No, the rule is that I can stay up until *eight* on weekends, except for *eight-thirty* when Nana is here." "We *always* open one present on Christmas Eve."
- Don't label them. It's a self-fulfilling prophecy. "The pretty one." "The smart one." "The underachiever." They're all different. Enjoy them for who they are.
- Don't ever say your child is "gifted" unless you're talking about Christmas.
- Little kids don't know the difference between good attention and bad attention. So find ways to reinforce *good* attention.
- Dr. Harriet Blumencranz quotes her daughter's pediatrician, Dr. Ramon Murphy, who says, "All bets are off if your child is hungry, sleepy, or sick."
- Laura's husband, Ray Menard, says that the four scariest words in the English language coming from a nursery-age child are: "I want to help." Once they're in middle school, the two scariest words are "school project."
- Let kids know you can fail. You're not perfect.
- You don't need to bring up how babies are made or why the man is wearing a dress unless your kids ask. And on the same theme, a preschool teacher says, "Don't explain everything over and over, going over *every* detail, just because *your* parents didn't explain anything."

- Don't be vague. "Don't spill" is clearer than "Be careful."
- You don't have to say "don't touch!" fifty times. Just say, "This is a looking store, not a touching store." This from all the parents who, for years, have convinced their children that FAO Schwarz is a toy museum, not a toy store.
- "When a three- or four-year-old makes big decisions, you're all in trouble," says a New York City kindergarten teacher. "They have way too much power and no limits."
- Kids have to win sometimes. A friend told me the story of her ten-year-old daughter calling her at the office. "Can I dye my hair red?" No, said her mother. The next day Gaby called again. "Can I paint my room black?" No. The next day, "Can I paint my nails black?" "Okay," her mother said, knowing that polish wears off and that it was fine for Gaby to feel in control.
- "We all want our children to be better than we are—and that's often what gets us going in the wrong direction," says a middle school social worker.
- Once is funny.
- The box is better than the toy. The bubble wrap is better than the box.
- Children are born knowing that lobster is better than fish sticks.
- Barbara Harrison suggests that when you go on vacation and leave your little kids with Grandma or a close friend, convince *them* that they are the ones taking the special vacation and you'll miss them very, very much. If they are over ten, don't mention "four-star luxury spa" or "Caribbean island."
- What's most important to know is that what they're learning, they are learning from you. Little kids aren't so attentive, but as they grow older, how you behave and the kind of role model you present are what count. The teaching is in the being. The simplest example is the parent who wants the child to read a book but never picks up a book.

- From a woman internist whose specialty is adolescent health: Even though you love them, there will be nights when you turn to your husband in bed and quietly say, "We should have had cats."

ADOPTION

New York literary agent Molly Friedrich has four children, two of them adopted. And she has a clear point of view about *why* and *when* to adopt. "If you adopt, do it because you want to love a child. Then do it with confidence."

SIBLINGS

- Phoebe's boyfriend Jake Danziger grew up with a friend named Isaac in Madison, Wisconsin. They both went to a wonderful, multiethnic, university-sponsored nursery school. Asked by his pregnant mother what kind of sibling he wanted, three-year-old Isaac replied, with conviction: "A black sister."

- When singer Wynonna Judd was asked about her sister, actress Ashley Judd, on *The Larry King Show*, Wynonna candidly admitted, "I'm like, you know, if I had known you were going to be this famous, I would have been really, really nice to you."

- "Some kids on some days are easier to love than others." —Laura Menard, mother of much-loved Amity and Isabel.

- How to space kids. A friend says, "Two years apart worked for me. Life was so chaotic, no one slept, so why not just keep it going. If I had waited until the first one was out of diapers or in school it would have been harder to start all over again." On the other hand, life surprises us.

- "Having twins—when you are forty-four—is not ideal," suggests my friend Nancy Stephens, who does admit that she knows more about the British rock scene and Kate Moss's wardrobe than just about any woman her age.

- "My first two kids I gave unusual names to," says my friend Marcell Greenfield. "Ina and Elliott. Then a friend said, 'Why don't you give them *normal* names,' so I named my third child Barbara. And of course only the third one complained. 'Why did you give me the name Barbara?' "

ON PREADOLESCENTS AND ADOLESCENTS

- The only time a teenager will ever tell you anything or confide something is when you are riding in a car with them. They're trapped with you and you are both looking straight ahead. Somehow it works.

- Don't expect logic. Or thanks. Fifteen-year-old Katie is going out for the evening with friends. She looks radiant as she leaves the house. "Have fun!" her mother says. "Don't tell me what to do!" Katie snarls.

- Mothers of teenagers know that at this complicated age, the best advice is simple: "When your kid is happy, you're happy."

- The second-best advice for mothers of teenage girls is, "When your teenager isn't strung out on drugs and/or eight months pregnant, you're *really* happy."

- If your child becomes a vegetarian or especially a vegan, buy firm tofu and a wok. Put away your beaver coat, crocodile bag, lizard pumps, and tortoiseshell bracelet. You'll be lucky if you can wear your leather shoes.

- "It's all about peer groups. By the time they are preadolescents they will have left you in the dust," says Phyllis Cohen, a psychotherapist whose practice includes many high school students and their parents. "So when they do talk to you, you'll be hearing a lot of 'gimme, I hate you, I have to have, I'll love you forever if you get me these jeans . . .' But," she says, "think of it as an arc of adjustment—with a beginning, middle, and end. A journey where things go up in the air and then come back down to earth. They grow up and find a place where they fit."

- A rule of thumb for parents of preteens: while your kid is trying on new friends and trying out new behaviors and not feeling comfortable in any situation, the best thing you can do is think of him or her as being on a trampoline. And you are the spotter—be there to catch them, guide them, buffer them, give them a reality check now and then. And don't be so anxious or rattled that it scares them.

- A friend who has four grown-up kids says, "Don't give up hope—they come back to you when they are in their early twenties. Happy, loving, caring, centered. They just need time to get launched. The separation and maturity take a while."

- Asked what's the right age to have kids, Barbara Harrison says, "Younger is better if you've found the right man. Menopause and adolescence should never share the same household."

- Stepparenting: give it at least ten years to work. And that's only if all involved (grown-ups) *really* try to make it positive; don't speak badly of each other; focus on what's best for the kids involved. And then, ultimately, what a wonderful payoff. My favorite was when my stepdaughter Megan was about twelve and I went to San Francisco on a business trip. She stayed with me in my fancy business hotel on Nob Hill where we could order room service and watch TV movies on our huge king-size bed. "Gosh," said one of the chambermaids the next morning, "the two of you really do look like mother and daughter." We both just smiled.

- A quick reminder to mothers of girls of how far we have to go. Media critic Nancy Franklin recently observed, "Boys aren't subject to the depredation of the Four Horsemen of Appropriateness—Received Notions About Femininity, Fear of Not Being Perceived as Nice, No Boy Will Ever Want You If You Act/Look/Talk Like That, and Caring Too Much What Other People Think of You."

PARENTING TIPS THAT WILL SAVE YOUR LIFE (OR AT LEAST YOUR SANITY)

Having children is the cure for smugness.

My friend Barbara Harrison says, "When all else fails, pull rank. When challenged one too many times with But *why*, Mommy, I resorted to 'Because I'm bigger, I'm older, and I own the place.' That worked for a while."

From my friend Dorothy Kalins: "Every mother is under the illusion that the *other* mothers are having meaningful talks with their children, that *other* children don't forget to bring *their* homework home and *volunteer* to help do the dishes. They don't."

Never have your children volunteer you for the lasagna entrée or the sheet cake for thirty. From day one, be the mother who supplies the paper cups and soft drinks, the napkins, the paper plates.

From Carol Ostrow, mother of four kids: "In airports everyone has to walk in front of me. When we are in an airport I want to keep my eyes on them. So I say, 'Airport rule!' and they run to get in front of me."

My friend Marcell relates the following: Three small rambunctious kids at home. A rainy day. Marcell's husband away on a business trip. Marcell, going a little crazy, called her pediatrician. "How about some wine?" he asked. Shocked, Marcell, said: "No, I can't give them *wine*!" "No, for you!" her pediatrician said. Marcell also admits to climbing under the dining room table to get a breather now and then.

A pragmatic mother says, "When you stop wishing something *could* be—if your husband *could* spend less time at work and more time with the kids; if your son *could* be less of a flake—it gets better."

Keep your sense of humor. Life has its absurdities.

THE REALITY

- Your daughter will *never* hate Barbie. Your son will play with trucks. Your daughter will insist on Malibu Barbie Spa. It will leak.

- You're the one that wanted wooden, hand-crafted "learning toys" and Museum of Modern Art mobiles for your child. Your house will be chockablock with large turquoise molded toys and your yard will be filled with plastic turtle sandboxes. And your child will actually prefer chocolate to granola.

- Even though you would prefer a homemade applesauce-sweetened cake with fresh lemon frosting, you will buy a Fudgie the Whale cake from Carvel.

- Your teenager will have a boyfriend or girlfriend you can't stand. Or can't understand. Phoebe, who was then around sixteen, started going out with a guy who was very sweet and polite—and to make it even better—she announced to us that Kevin didn't drink. "That's great!" I said, loving this kid already. "Uh-huh, he's in AA," she said. And then, just a few years later she had another boyfriend, who I think was a sophomore in college; he was soft-spoken and bright. Both my then-husband and I liked him a lot. One gorgeous day, we were all sitting on our terrace with the sun shining as we lingered over brunch and cappuccino. "Gosh," Ricky said, "This is so beautiful and quiet." Pause. "It reminds me of a detox center."

PETS

- Flushable pets, like fish, are easier. Although we did have one huge goldfish who jumped out of the bowl one day onto the kitchen floor, in what seemed like nothing less than a successful suicide bid. Try explaining *that*.

- On the other hand, by the time they are in nursery school, kids have figured out that things with fur on them are more fun. People ask, how do you know when your child is ready for a cat or dog or a bunny? I only know when they're *not* ready. When Phoebe was three, we got a cat. Phoebe loved the cat but "didn't quite understand how to handle him" (that's a bit of a euphemism). Once, when it was *way* too quiet in the living room, I called out "What are you doing?" And Phoebe answered, "I'm arranging the cat." Those aren't words you want to hear. I raced in to see that she was sitting right on top of the cat and extricated him. I just felt relieved it wasn't a small nonfurry sibling.

- The Law of Pets: The dog or cat will *always* poop/ pee/throw up/expel a fur ball on the antique Oriental rug and *never* on the bare wood floor. Corollary: Your child will *always* drool/throw up/projectile vomit on cashmere/ silk/fur.

- Just say no to: custom-made, imported canopied dog beds; Hermès collars and leashes for dogs. Spas for cats.

- When you get a puppy or newborn kitty, it is wise to give it a neutral name. Phoebe named her two-week-old kitty Benjamin (the pet store owner said it was male), only to find out at the kitty's first checkup that Benjamin was a female. Another friend named her puppy Macbeth only to discover Macbeth was female. But at least in that case, she could just adjust the name to Lady Macbeth. The hardest pets to tell the sex of are rabbits. Children are easier.

- And on the note of naming pets, do not let your child name the goldfish after a family member. My colleague Garrick has a nephew named Andrew who did just that with his three fish, naming them Uncle Garrick, Uncle Gregory, and Aunt Sharon. It all worked great until the morning Andrew woke up and saw that one fish had died in the night. "Daddy, Daddy!" he cried, running into his parents' room. "Wake up! Uncle Gregory died!"

FIVE

You Can Never Go Wrong
with a Roast Chicken

"Life's a banquet and most poor suckers are starving to death."

—Auntie Mame

First of all, there's way too much *information*— zillions of books and articles and websites and newsletters and Food Network shows about how and what to eat; how to cook; how to entertain; the right pot; the wrong knives; the critical importance of *un*salted butter; the *correct* height for the centerpiece; the precise ripeness of the chevre; exactly how long the cocktail part of the dinner party should last. *Dictates:* "Cooking is an *art,* baking is a *science.*" Add to *that* the *advice* of well-meaning mothers and aunts and grandmas and friends who have their *own* techniques, their *own* biases, their *own* repertoire of dishes, their *own* opinions. Let's put it this way: too many cooks spoil the fun.

Second, there's way too much disagreement and contradiction. Try to get three foodies to agree on the best way to mash potatoes, the right technique for making risotto, what to coat the chicken with before you fry it, and what wine really compliments Moo Shu

Duck. These days, spatulas are usually far more flexible than most serious cooks.

It's not only enough to make a person crazy, it's enough to make you scared to death to even go into the kitchen and *try* to cook something. For a novice, it makes the idea of throwing a dinner party about as appealing as being asked to perform a triple bypass or drive a rental car in Rome.

Is it any coincidence that so many food terms have to do with feeling defeated? *Beaten* biscuits; *whipped* cream; *creamed* corn; *sour* cream; a recipe for *smashed* potatoes with *crushed* black olives. Then there's *flounder* and *fool*. Not to mention this obscure and oddly sad cooking directive: "First, *muddle* the strawberries."

Take heart. No matter what your level of skill, lack of skill, or level of apprehension, you will take away three important things from this chapter.

> **First Important Thing:** It's really pretty easy—once you get the hang of it—to make a delicious dinner or host a terrific party. You need to know the basics, get some good advice, and have enough experience to gain a little confidence.
>
> **Second Important Thing:** It's supposed to be *fun*. Not torture. Not a test of your self-worth. Eight brilliant words from British food authority Shirley Conran: "Life is too short to stuff a mushroom."
>
> **Third Important Thing:** Always wear shoes when you are cooking so if you drop the sharp knife you are using you will not amputate a toe. My cooking philosophy: Many triumphs. A few flops. No flip-flops.

I believe that if they can condense soup, I can condense this vast and overwhelming area of ingredients, recipes, cookware, cookbooks, home cooking, dinner parties, cheese, wine, and dining out. I can help you separate the rules you need to follow from the ones you should feel free to break. I'll help you recognize the experts you can count on for sound advice, good cheer, and recipes that live up to their descriptions and your expectations. That way you can turn cooking and entertaining into what they should be: delicious, satisfying experiences that give great pleasure to you and the people you love.

There is a category of sensational writers—they're pitch perfect whether they're writing about food or life. They combine food and life wisdom in equal parts and have a voice all their own: Laurie Colwin, Ruth Reichl, Anna Thomas, Nigella Lawson, Edna Lewis, Alice Waters. (All women . . . hmm.)

There are international stars who will introduce you to a whole world of tastes and possibilities. Patricia Wells on everything French, the Italian family dynasty of Marcella Hazan, her husband Victor Hazan (who specializes in writing about Italian wine), and their gifted son Giuliano Hazan. The accomplished Marian Cunningham. Of course, Julia Child, who first introduced classical French cooking into American kitchens. The champion of authentic American food, James Beard. Paula Wolfert, who makes an exotic Mediterranean cuisine both accessible and dazzling. And for exploring and demystifying the world of Asian food, Corinne Trang.

There are contemporary writers who will steer you to the tastes and lifestyle we are looking for today. There's Mark Bittman (*How to Cook Everything*), John Willoughby and Chris Schlesinger (*The Thrill of the Grill*), Deborah Madison (*The Greens Cookbook, Vegetarian Cooking for Everyone*), Pamela Anderson (*The Perfect Recipe*), and Colman Andrews (editor of *Saveur* magazine and author, with contributors, of *Saveur Cooks Authentic American*).

And if you're just starting out, an easy but elegant cookbook that lets you wow your guests without spending a fortune is *The $50 Dinner Party*, by Sally Sampson.

The Cake Bible, by Rose Levy Beranbaum, is the most comprehensive step-by-step guide to everything from a simple fondant icing to a Blueberry Swan Lake cake with meringue swans a-swimming. A classic book—surprisingly user-friendly and one you'll turn to again and again—is Maida Heatter's *Book of Great Desserts*. A testimony to its popularity is the fact that every single review on amazon.com gives it five stars and raves.

A book to make you smarter than any barista: Corby Kummer's comprehensive *The Joy of Coffee*.

While no Alice Waters, my credentials for this chapter include heavy duty on the home front—cooking breakfast, lunch, and dinner for my family for over twenty years and not once ordering in from Domino's.

I did not come from a food family. In fact, the two things my mother taught me were how to make an okay baked ham and how to get the most out of an electric can opener. But thanks to my love of food, going to good restaurants, having friends who were excellent cooks, and also taking some cooking courses, I was eventually plowing through Julia Child and mastering the art of just about everything *except* electric can openers. But even then, I balked at attempting some techniques. Until very recently (and I've never shared this with anyone) *caramelizing* was a huge Food Fear Factor for me. For years I lived without the rich homemade caramel icing that would have made my yellow cake dazzle, and as much as I wanted to try the recipe for fresh peaches in a warm caramel sauce, I just couldn't. (Oddly enough, I never had *any* fears about baking beaten biscuits, but mine came out rock hard or rubbery every single time, so I *should* have had a lot of fear about that.)

But one day I said to myself, "If you could go through *twenty-three hours* of labor and a forceps delivery with *no* drugs, you can caramelize." And I took out the sugar and cast-iron pan and just did it. Now of course you can't stop me. The point is we all find some techniques too tricky or some foods too weird to try. So my advice is that if you have a deep-seated and irrational fear of something like cleaning raw squid or making a meringue, just think about two profoundly personal things in your life—like forceps and caramel icing—that together will inspire you to succeed beyond your wildest dreams. Or take a cooking class.

KITCHEN WISDOM: WE'VE COOKED IT, SERVED IT, OBSERVED IT

The first three are from my friend Barbara Harrison, who could have written this book herself. (Hey, she *sort* of did.)

- "No woman ever eats a whole *anything*. Cut the brownies and lemon squares in half."

- "Clean the house after the guests leave rather than before they arrive. The exception is the bathrooms, which do have to be clean and sparkly. But if you keep the lights low, use candles, and stuff the clutter in a back room or closet, no one will notice (or care) if you vacuumed or polished in advance."

- "Serve things you can prepare ahead. What's the point of having friends over if you're stuck in the kitchen chopping, measuring, or mixing?"

- Patty Thomson, who owns the popular New York Mexican restaurant Mexicana Mama: "When men order at a restaurant, they order what's on the menu. Women insist on substitutions." See if this sounds familiar: "Can you hold the mayo?" "I want the salad dressing on the side . . . no, just bring me a few lemon wedges." "Can you substitute vegetables for the potatoes?" "Can you make the sushi with *brown* rice?"

- On dinner parties, from a friend who is extremely pragmatic: "Never ask, 'Is there anything you can't/don't eat?' because these days everyone will tell you. That's why we have restaurants. If it's your house, it's your menu."

- Sometimes store-bought is just fine. When my then-husband and I first moved to the suburbs, we got invited to a neighborhood potluck supper. Everyone was asked to bring a dish; I brought a butternut squash casserole that I had seen in *Gourmet*. It took me almost four hours to make—cutting, dicing, and roasting the squash; making a béchamel sauce; chopping fresh herbs. When all the dishes were spread out on the candlelit table for supper, I noticed that my neighbor

71

Lynn's contribution was a large smoked salmon that she had bought and simply put on a pretty platter with lemon slices. "Wow," someone said, "that salmon is *terrific!*" "Smoked salmon . . . mmm . . ." someone else said. "What's this?" asked a woman about my dish. "Looks like some kind of casserole. It's so dark I can't see it," her husband responded.

- A friend has a similar story. At a gourmet potluck lunch, she chose to bring a large bowl of her homemade macaroni and cheese along with a cake made from the recipe on the back of the Hershey's cocoa box. They were the hit of the night.

- Fondon'ts: Double-dipping. Ick.

- Don't let restaurant service throw you. When your lovely Japanese waitress suggests the special of "boiled rabbi," just order the chicken teriyaki.

WINE

"Wine in. Secret out."—Old French proverb

Tipsy guests are okay, but a tipsy hostess is never adorable.

Wine, like cheese and fish, can be extraordinarily bewildering. Do not despair. And if you are new at this, you are not destined for a life where you automatically say, "I'll have the Merlot" or "I'll have the Chardonnay" and never ask for the wine that you think you might like but can't pronounce. I'm not sure there are Fish Snobs, but there are definitely Wine Snobs who act as both Wine Police and insufferable know-it-alls.

Cheers to wine expert Scott Pactor (www.appelationnyc.com) for his help.

- Wine should not be scary. Finding a store with a helpful staff or a restaurant with a sommelier whom you can trust is key.

- When you're at a wine store, you should be able to describe the type of wine you like, how much you want to spend, and what food you will eat with the wine. And how adventurous are you? Do you want to try something new? Something from Chile or Argentina, something sparkling, something sweet when you usually like dry? Bare your soul.

- Go to wine tastings—most good wine stores have them. Get on a mailing list. As with cheese, you need to sample and learn and, oh, have fun discovering what you like. Take a wine course. I did and it was fantastic. Plus it's the one course where the homework is a pleasure.

- In a restaurant with a progressive list, the wines will be listed from light to full. So if you like a full-bodied Chardonnay, those wines will be listed toward the bottom.

- Just like in a foreign restaurant where you are clueless, "point and request" works. Just point to something on the wine list and ask the waiter or sommelier to tell you about it and its characteristics. She or he will say the name for you.

- Whites should be served around 50 degrees Fahrenheit and reds are always served at room temperature. Room temperature is considered to be around 60 degrees.

- To send back or not? If you hate the bottle or glass, have the waiter or sommelier try it. They should be able to determine if it is flawed. If it's not, then an amenable place will usually try to determine what you didn't like and bring you another selection. If you ordered a *really* expensive wine, don't expect such flexibility from the staff.

- When matching food and wine, many professionals will use weight as their primary guide. A light Muscadet, for example, will be paired with a light fish. A heavier, oilier fish will go better with a fuller-bodied wine such as a big white Burgundy.

- Don't save sparkling wine for celebrations. And don't just go for champagne. There's California sparkling like Chandon, Italian Prosecco, and Spanish Cava. And what makes it really worth celebrating is that none of these wines has to cost a fortune.

• If not stored properly, wine turns to vinegar. Keep it cool in your house and it will be happy. Build a major temperature-controlled cellar in your house. (Kidding.) If you have central air, store your wine on its side in a cool, dark place. If you have a window air conditioner and can't guarantee it will stay cool on a continual basis, you can keep both reds and whites in the refrigerator. Just take the red out about thirty minutes before opening.

Great Wines You Can Buy Anywhere and Won't Break the Bank

The wine may be rich, but you don't have to be. You also don't need to be in New York or Napa to find something terrific.
—From wine expert Tomek Koszylko, who worked at one of New York's most venerable liquor stores:

"You can buy these wines pretty much anywhere in the country. I've divided them into two groups: 'Wines Under $15' and 'Wines Under $25.' (Some of these prices may have gone up by the time this gets published—sorry.) The first group is a good bet for everyday dinners or just a 'sipping wine' to have at home. There might be a few wines on the list that don't make it to every corner of the country, but 90 percent of them should be readily available. The remaining 10 percent can be purchased over the phone or on the internet." (Unless you are unlucky enough to live in Tennessee, Florida, or about eight other states that don't allow the mailing of wine.)

Great Wines Under $15

Reds

Kendall-Jackson: Their Merlot or Cabarnet Sauvignon are great, easy-drinking wines: the producer is very consistent from year to

---

year. Even if it's a poor year for California reds, Kendall-Jackson, on account of its size, is able to produce a consistently good product. Both wines are smooth and pair well with food.

Los Vascos (Chile): This is a winemaker that produces outstanding values in wine. The vineyards are owned by the Rothschild family, which owns some of the greatest, most expensive Bordeaux estates in France. You'll find a Los Vascos Cabernet Sauvignon for under $10, and they have a Reserve bottle of Cabernet for under $18, a few dollars more but worth mentioning because it makes a great gift bottle. The Cab is full-bodied and rich, and the Reserve is much, much better than its price tag. If you can't find Los Vascos, try other Chilean winemakers, like Undurraga or Santa Rita (see below).

Santa Rita: The Santa Rita "120" Cabernet is a good example of how well the Cabernet grape does in Chile. The wine is delicious and soft, yet it has good substance and surprisingly complex palate textures. It has a long finish (you taste its essence after you've swallowed the wine).

Duboeuf: Georges Duboeuf is the largest producer of Beaujolais in France. Duboeuf makes dozens of different wines. Each wine is named after the town where the grape is produced. You'll find Beaujolais Villages, Régnié, Brouilly, Saint Amour, Morgon, and Moulin à Vent. The most common Duboeuf reds are the Beaujolais and Beaujolais Villages. They're fruity, smooth, and very easy to drink. Drink them with red meat or chicken. They also make great gift bottles, because the labels are pretty and, let's face it, French wine is impressive, even if it costs $12.

St. Francis: This California winemaker makes a great selection of wines, most of which cost around $15. Great big fruit with a good dose of oak in the Cabernet; the Merlot is also delicious.

Yellow Tail: This Australian wine is wonderful. It's very inexpensive (most bottles cost under $8), and it has great flavor. They make a lovely Shiraz, which is both fruity and peppery. It goes well with roast red meats, like steak or lamb chops. Also look for the Cabernet

Sauvignon, and less frequently, the Merlot. The Cab is good with roast red meats, while the Merlot is wonderful with lighter meats like pork, chicken, or even salmon.

White Wines

Sterling: Sterling has both a Chardonnay and a Sauvignon Blanc for around $12. The Chardonnay is a bigger, oakier wine with a smoother flavor. It goes well with fish or chicken. The Sauvignon Blanc is grassier, drier, and works well with the same meats mentioned above.

Simi: Simi is a wonderful winemaker. Their white wines cost around $13 to $14. The Chardonnays have the soft flavors of melon and tropical fruit, while the Sauvignon Blanc wine tastes grassy, with flavors of pineapple and lemon. Have the Chardonnay with chicken or salmon, and the Sauvignon Blanc with light fish, like flounder.

Undurraga: Another wonderful Chilean winemaker. Their white wines will cost between $6 and $9. Again, the flavors that dominate the Chardonnay are melon and soft pitted fruit like peaches. The Sauvignon Blanc tastes more tropical with a sharper edge.

Duboeuf: Yes, Georges Duboeuf also makes white wines. Taste his Beaujolais Blanc, Mâcon Villages, Pouilly Fuissé. They're Chardonnay-based white wines, but they're surprisingly crisp and light. Price: around $10 to $15.

Edna Valley: Delicious Chardonnay and Sauvignon Blanc. Both around $12—an excellent value for a California white. The Chardonnay is refreshing, with tropical fruit and mineral accents, while the Sauvignon Blanc is a fruity, peachy, citrusy white.

Great Wines Under $25

Reds

Chateau Ste. Michelle: This Washington State label makes great reds. The Cabernet and the Merlot cost between $16 and $18. A good value for a quality wine.

Robert Mondavi: Mondavi makes wines that cost between $6 and $100. Consider these great gift wines for any price range. Check out the Merlot, Pinot Noir, and Cabernet Sauvignon, all for around $20 a bottle. The Reserves will cost you quite a bit more, about $100 a bottle. But a great corporate gift, if that's what you need.

Francis Coppola: Diamond Series Merlot and Claret Red Wines. Both offer a great value for between $15 and $18 a bottle. The Merlot is fruity and easy to drink, while the Claret blend is a classic Bordeaux blend; smoky, berry-heavy, and spicy, with a rich, burgundy-purple color.

Catena: This winemaker from Argentina makes a Malbec for around $20. If you like Cabernet Sauvignon, you'll love Malbec, which has a big berry flavor complemented with a backbone of warm spice and toasted oak.

Errazuriz: Another great Chilean winemaker. Look for their Reserve Cabernet Sauvignon and Reserve Syrah for a good $20 bottle.

Whites

Louis Jadot: Look for Louis Jadot's Pouilly Fuissé for an exquisite white wine. It's an un-oaked Chardonnay, full of flavor but still light and minerally. For a $12 bottle, get Jadot's Mâcon Villages.

Robert Mondavi: Mondavi's whites are as good as his reds. The Fumé Blanc is a dry, crisp white wine for people who love Sauvignon Blanc. The Carneros Chardonnay is beautifully balanced, soft, and hinting of melon and peaches.

Santa Margherita: Very light and fruity and very easy to drink. About $20.

Francis Coppola: Diamond Series Chardonnay is big and full of flavor, with hints of apple, lemon, and tropical fruit. It's a great value at around $15.

Trimbach: This French winemaker from the Alsace region makes a delicious Pinot Gris, which is the name the French give to Pinot Grigio. Bigger and fuller bodied than a Pinot Grigio, the Pinot Gris is dry and full of soft peach and apricot notes. It goes great with all kinds of food.

ENTERTAINING

- Plan ahead, keep it simple, don't try something new for your guests unless you are a thrill seeker.

- If the music is too loud, it will drown out any conversation. If it is too soft, no one will hear it. If it is opera, someone will hate opera. If it's Sondheim, there will be too many songs about failed marriages and sour relationships. No to the harpsichord or organ or symphonies with fireworks. Try jazz or lounge music or samba or upbeat Coldplay or Fountains of Wayne or French rock or mixes you've made yourself.

- When there are more than six people, a round table makes sense. You can see everyone, talk to everyone, and have one conversation going.

- *Unscented* candles for softer lighting and a festive look. Always. Lots of them. Tea candles, votives, tapers.

- Six little glass vases filled with fresh lilies of the valley look better on the table than a random mixture of flowers and vases. Twenty green apples in a big white bowl look fabulous. Ditto a dozen miniature white pumpkins on an antique Drabware platter. Low centerpieces so you can see across the table. Just skim through any two issues of *Martha Stewart Living* and you get it.

- Roasts—especially rib roasts and roast beef—sound easy but are deceptively hard to do for dinner parties. First of all, you'll be hysterical with the $75.00 computerized meat thermometer obsessively checking to see if it's done. (Overcooking the meat and not having enough food are two of the scariest things about dinner parties, even for experienced party givers.) Then, perversely, everyone at the table will like their roast cooked differently—rare, well done, medium, slightly blue, crusty. Good luck.

CHEESES

Cheers to Paula Lambert from the Mozzarella Company (www.mozzco.com) in Dallas for her help.

- Cheese before or after dinner? If you're a cheese lover, any time is great. In America we tend to offer cheese as an hors d'oeuvre along with nuts and olives or with fruits like pears, apples, grapes.

- Crackers and bread for the cheese are best plain, rather than flavored. Ms. Lambert says, "There are exceptions: olive bread, for instance, is wonderful with a fresh mozzarella or a goat cheese." Joël Robuchon (in the book *French Cheeses*) advises: "The more delicate the cheese, the whiter and less salted ought to be the bread that goes with it."

- Cheese should *always* be at room temperature.

- The optimum number of cheeses for a cheese tray is from three to five of contrasting flavors. A good selection would be a cheddar, a brie, a goat cheese with herbs.

- Some cheeses not to commute with or leave in your car when it's parked in the sun: Limburger, Epoisse, a pungent chevre.

- If a cheese is overripe when you get it home, go back and return it. One way to avoid this is to find a cheese store or department you trust. Ask them what's good that day. Often a cheese gets stronger and stronger as it ages—what you want to avoid is an odor or flavor of ammonia.

- Soft-ripening cheeses like Brie and Camembert ripen from the edges inward. Feel the cheese in the center when you buy it. Sometimes pasteurized, industrially produced bries and Camemberts never soften. Again, trust your instincts or talk to someone about the condition and ripeness.

- Artisanal cheeses are far superior to factory-made cheeses. President Camembert is an example of a mass-produced Camembert that, like a factory-grown U.S. tomato, is bred more for its sturdiness than for its taste. Cowgirl Creamery, Coach Farms, Vermont Butter & Cheese are three artisanal cheese makers whose products are widely available.

- This—and I couldn't make it up—from Ms. Lambert: "One way to judge ripeness is to put one finger on your closed eyeball and another on the center of the cheese. They should be about the same softness." I'm not sure how this would go over in a cheese store in Paris or New York, but Dallas is probably a lot more forgiving.

- Read a great encyclopedic cheese book or take a cheese class. General cookbooks like Deborah Madison's and Mark Bittman's have helpful sections on cheese.

- "Can I please have a taste?" is the way to go in a well-stocked cheese store like Murray's in New York or Whole Foods or Zingerman's in Ann Arbor. Since there are about a zillion cheeses to choose from, new ones being introduced all the time, and because it's so rewarding to keep educating yourself, try all sorts of different kinds.

TWENTY IMPORTANT (OR AT LEAST SURPRISING) THINGS ABOUT FOOD

- The chicken is done when the juice runs clear.

- Any baking recipe that calls for eggs means "large" eggs. (Because baking is so precise, extra large eggs won't work.)

- Hollandaise sauce is nothing more than cooked mayonnaise made with good butter. Don't worry because it is so fattening that almost nobody eats it anymore.

- You can't always just double or triple a recipe and expect it to work. Two brownie pans in one oven, for example, are likely to make the brownies burn on the side. When you're roasting vegetables the pan needs to be big enough for the vegetables to have space between them—so if you double the recipe, you can't pile them all into the same size pan and expect them to get nice and crisp.

- The key to grilling meat is to keep it from drying out. So if you're making kebabs, whether it's lamb, pork, or beef, make the chunks large. This way, exteriors can brown before the interiors dry out.

- When you're grilling chicken, never grill breasts (not even boneless—even though a lot of recipes say you can). They dry out no matter how little you cook them or how much you marinate them.

- The only frozen vegetables that can easily substitute for fresh are spinach and peas. And sometimes corn.

- Mountain Gorgonzola is the best blue cheese for salads, like a classic endive, walnut, and blue cheese salad. Unlike sweet Italian Gorgonzola or Saga blue, it's not too creamy to crumble. Also, it's not too dry, too sharp, or too overpowering.

- You really never *can* go wrong with a roast chicken. It is comfort food; it is delicious; it is simple; it is easy to make; we all grew up with it; no one doesn't like it; it gets to go with mashed potatoes and cranberries and all the other things we all love.

- People either hate or love: brussels sprouts, snails, sweetbreads, marzipan, liver, cilantro, eel, sardines, beets. They either will or will not eat foie gras, veal, rabbit, or wild game. One more reason to serve roast chicken.

- By the end of June no one wants to see another zucchini.

- If a melon sounds hollow when you tap it, it's ripe. Smell the end and if it's fragrant, that confirms it.

- While these classic American fruit desserts are very similar, there are *real* differences between a "cobbler," a "crisp," a "fool," a "dowdy," "a grunt," a "buckle," and a "Brown Betty." But nobody really cares.

- No one really knows the difference between yams and sweet potatoes.

- If you want to entertain your guests after dinner, microwave Peeps.

- Never order fish in a restaurant on Sunday.
- While vegetarians can't eat meat, they can eat animal crackers. Vegans eat no meat, no fish, no dairy. Since I had my own vegan at home, my definition of vegan is: "Whatever you're cooking, they can't eat it."
- Never marinate fish for more than an hour. It will get mushy.
- The lifespan for leftovers in your refrigerator is three to five days.
- Never apologize for something you've cooked, even if you know it's not your best. All that does is make your guests have to reassure you that, "no, it's terrific . . . really," while giving them a reason to doubt their own taste.

THE BARE MINIMUM

You'll never go hungry if you have the following staples on hand:

- Pasta and rice
- Canned beans; canned tomatoes
- Dried herbs and spices
- Olive oil, vinegar, and soy sauce
- Eggs and butter
- Flour and cornmeal
- Nuts and dried fruits
- Onions, potatoes, garlic, carrots, celery
- Nonfat dry milk (usually for emergencies)
- Canned stock
- Different types of mustard
- Canned Italian tuna
- A jar of French cornichon pickles
- A loaf of great grain-y bread in your freezer—all you need is to pick up some cheddar on the way home and you can make a satisfying grilled cheese sandwich

- Frozen pesto sauce
- A few bottles of wine
- The phone number of the Chinese take-out place

MUST HAVES: RECIPES

The following are recipes for six classics that always work and always satisfy and are always winners. They are great whether it's two of you or six, a weeknight at home or a dinner party.

- Macaroni and cheese
- Brownies
- Roast chicken
- Martini
- Sangria
- Green salad and dressing

Home-Style Macaroni and Cheese

This always makes the creamiest, yummiest macaroni and cheese. Make sure you use really good cheddar—it makes a *big* difference.

Salt
$\frac{1}{2}$ pound elbow macaroni or DeCecco cavatappi
4 tablespoons salted butter
$\frac{1}{4}$ cup all purpose flour
1 tablespoon dry mustard
3 cups milk
3 drops Tabasco
1 teaspoon Worcestershire sauce
1 pound sharp cheddar, grated
1 to $1\frac{1}{2}$ cups of cooked, cubed ham

1. Preheat oven to 350 degrees.
2. Butter an 8-inch baking dish.
3. In a pot of lightly salted boiling water, add pasta and cook until al dente. Drain pasta and rinse with cool running water. Drain and set aside.

4. In a medium-sized saucepan melt the butter until it foams. Take saucepan off heat and whisk in flour. Return pan to stove. Over moderate heat, whisk until the mixture begins to bubble, about 3 minutes. Whisk in mustard. Add the milk in a steady stream, whisking continuously.

5. Turn heat up to high and keep whisking until the mixture comes to a boil. Once it bubbles and begins to thicken, about 10 minutes, let it boil for an additional 3 minutes, stirring constantly.

6. Remove the pan from the stove, and add the Tabasco and Worcestershire. Add about three-quarters of the cheese and stir until blended and smooth. Add the ham.

7. Combine pasta with the ham and cheese mixture and pour into baking dish. Sprinkle remaining cheese on top and bake for 30 minutes.

If you want a browner top, broil on high for 1 minute until it's golden.

Cynthia's Sugar-Kissed Brownies
BY CYNTHIA CARR GARDNER

$^3/_4$ cup unsalted butter

4 ounces good quality unsweetened chocolate (Baker's will do)

2 cups sugar

3 eggs, beaten slightly

Pinch of salt

1 teaspoon vanilla extract or Espresso

1 cup flour

6 to 8 tablespoons of sugar

1. Preheat oven to 350 degrees.

2. Spray a 13 x 9-inch pan with cooking spray or grease the pan with butter, then lightly flour.

3. Melt the butter and chocolate in a microwave-safe bowl on high for 30 seconds at a time, stirring in between, until melted, approximately a minute and a half. Stir until completely melted/blended. Let cool slightly.

4. Fold in the sugar until incorporated.

5. Add eggs, salt, and vanilla, gently stirring until well blended.

6. Add flour, mixing just to incorporate. Do not overmix.

7. Scrape the batter into the prepared pan. Bake for 30 to 35 minutes.

Brownies will have a slightly dull finish, puff up a bit, and feel semisolid to a light touch. Do not overbake.

8. Remove from oven and immediately dust with 6 to 8 tablespoons sugar. Gently shake the pan from side to side and back and forth to cover the top of the brownies completely with sugar. Tip pan and carefully pour off excess sugar. The warm brownies will melt the sugar slightly, making it adhere nicely, forming a slightly crunchy sugar coating. Dresses them up a bit!

9. Let brownies cool completely. Cut them into however many squares desired. For a fancier treatment, use a serrated knife and cut off perimeter of brownies to make a crustless batch.

Foolproof Roast Chicken
BY CHRISTOPHER HIRSHEIMER, FOOD WRITER AND PHOTOGRAPHER

There are only a few things in life that are really helpful to know, and one of them is that you should always cut the back out of a chicken before you roast it. It will make for much easier carving. The chicken can be, as the English say, spatchcocked (cooked flat) or re-formed into a round chicken shape. While slathering the bird with olive oil or butter is very delicious, the skin will be crispier if you cook it *au naturel*.

Serves 4

3 pounds or larger organic chicken
Salt and freshly ground black pepper

1. Preheat the oven to 450 degrees.
2. Use poultry shears or a sharp heavy knife (be careful!) to remove the back by cutting along both sides of the backbone. (Save the back and throw it, along with the neck, gizzards, heart, a rib of celery, a small carrot, and a halved onion into a pot with 4 cups of water. Add a pinch of salt and a few peppercorns. Simmer slowly over low heat for about an hour, then raise heat to reduce the stock to about a cup. Strain and use to make a little gravy with the pan drippings.)
3. Rinse the chicken, then pat dry with paper towels. Put the chicken in a large roasting pan and season liberally with salt and pepper. This minimizes clean up *and* seasons the drippings.
4. Lay the bird flat on a rack in the pan or re-form it into a round, natural

shape of a chicken (albeit one without a backbone, not a very stand-up sort of chicken) and tie the legs together with kitchen string.

5. Add 1 cup of water to the pan; this will keep the pan juices from drying up and burning.

6. Put the chicken in the oven and roast for 1 hour without opening the door and peeking. If you have the courage, it is even better if you roast the bird at 500 degrees. But such a high temperature makes a lot of people nervous (and can cause an oven fire if your oven isn't clean).

7. Remove the pan from the oven. Remove the chicken to a platter and allow the bird to rest for 15 minutes to collect itself and reabsorb all the tasty juices before you serve it. This will give you a chance to make a little gravy with the stock you made.

8. Add the stock to the pan. On top of the stove over medium heat, bring the stock to a simmer, using a rubber spatula or a wooden spoon to loosen all the delicious, brown crusty bits stuck to the bottom of the pan. Taste, and season with salt and pepper if needed. Serve with the chicken.

The Perfect Martini

Serves 1

Splash of dry vermouth
Olives (1 to 3 is traditional) or lemon peel
6 ounces gin or vodka
Ice (cubes will work, crushed is better)

1. Start by refrigerating your vermouth for the amount of time it takes for the bottle to get cold (at least an hour). Chill a martini glass in the refrigerator or the freezer for about 10 minutes.

2. Take the frosted glass out and pour a small amount of vermouth into it. Here's the important bit: swirl the vermouth in the glass so that the sides of the glass are coated. DISCARD THE REMAINING VERMOUTH.

3. Spear an olive (or two, or three), and put it in the glass.

4. Pour your gin or vodka into a shaker over copious amounts of ice. Gently stir so as not to bruise the alcohol.

5. Strain into the glass, and you're good to go.

Note: There are those people who would nix the vermouth altogether in a martini. It reminds me of Winston Churchill's martini recipe:

1. Pour gin in glass.
2. Look at a bottle of vermouth.
3. Drink.

Enjoy.

White Zinfandel Sangria

My friend Betsy got married in what was "the Year of the Punch Bowl." She says that finding a really delicious sangria recipe started out as a way to use one of the three punch bowls she got. It's fresh, easy, and packs a nice punch (pun intended).

Serves 6

750-milliliter bottle of chilled white zinfandel
½ cup of peach schnapps
2 tablespoons of Cointreau or other orange liqueur
2 tablespoons of sugar
2 cinnamon sticks, broken in half
Lemon, sliced
Orange, sliced
Peach, sliced into wedges
10-ounce bottle of chilled club soda
Ice cubes

1. Mix first 8 ingredients in tall pitcher. Refrigerate at least 30 minutes to allow flavors to blend.
2. Mix in club soda.
3. Fill six wineglasses with ice cubes. Pour sangria over ice and serve.

The Perfect Salad and Dressing

BY CHRISTOPHER HIRSHEIMER, FOOD WRITER AND PHOTOGRAPHER

I like a ratio of 1 part acid to 4 parts oil in my salad dressing, but make it according to your own taste. Lemon juice is nice to use because it doesn't fight with wine (and that could be ugly), but you can substitute any vinegar if you prefer.

Serves 2 to 4

For the salad:
Lots of different young lettuces

For the dressing:
1 small garlic clove, peeled and minced
1 anchovy filet or a small dollop of anchovy paste
Salt
Juice of half a lemon, more if you like
$\frac{1}{4}$ cup extra-virgin olive oil
Freshly ground black pepper
Handful of parsley leaves, finely chopped

1. Wash the lettuce in a large bowl or a sink full of cold water, lifting the leaves out of the water, allowing any dirt to settle on the bottom. Shake off any water from the leaves or use a salad spinner. Wrap the leaves in paper towels, then store them in plastic bags in the refrigerator. Greens can be prepared several days ahead of use.
2. Mash the garlic and anchovy together with a mortar and pestle or puree in a food processor. (You can also simply use a heavy knife to chop and mash the anchovy garlic and parsley together on a cutting board. A little kosher salt on the board will add "grit," which will help the chopping process. Then transfer to a small bowl and continue.)
3. Add the lemon juice and oil, whisking everything together until emulsi-fied. Add more oil or lemon juice to suit your taste.
4. Season to taste with salt and pepper.
5. Stir in the chopped parsley.
6. Pour the dressing into a large salad bowl. Put your greens on top and bring the whole thing to the table, but don't mix until you are ready to serve.

A Roast Chicken Joke (and You Don't See Many of *These*)

A guy had a pet parrot who swore like a sailor. The guy loved the parrot but he couldn't take it anymore. So he asked the parrot to stop swearing. All the parrot did was to cuss even louder and more often. So the man spoke to the parrot again and said, "This *has* to stop. No more swearing." "You . . . you're a piece of * * * *!!!!!!," the parrot yelled at the top of his lungs and the guy couldn't take it for one more minute. He picked up the screaming parrot, opened the freezer door, and stuck him inside. Fifteen minutes later, the guy started to feel absolutely awful about what he had done. So he raced into the kitchen and opened the freezer door. To his surprise and delight, the parrot was very much alive. "I'm so sorry," said the parrot, "I'll never swear again." "No," said this owner, "*I'm* sorry. I hope you'll forgive me for doing that to you!" "Oh I do," said the contrite parrot. "But," the parrot continued, "could I ask you a question?" "Sure," said the guy. "Well," said the parrot, "what did the *chicken* do?"

HERE'S A SHORT LIST OF WEBSITES FOR FOODIES

www.epicurious.com: The king of all food websites, it has recipes galore, articles, restaurant guides, pictures of how dishes are prepared, a search engine that brings up myriad recipes that include a specific ingredient, and food and wine dictionaries if the recipes stump you.

www.asiafood.org: A comprehensive site for all Asian food, searchable by ingredient (there's a glossary, too), technique, or equipment. Also has great articles highlighting various regions and foods.

www.foodreference.com: Devoted to the culture of food more than the preparation, this site has much fun information you'd be hard-pressed to find elsewhere. From food quotes to poems and art about food, you'll go in curious and come out hours later knowing that the blueberry muffin is the official muffin of Minnesota.

www.globaltable.com: Where to find the perfect bowl or platter or serving spoons. Chic and contemporary and nothing fussy or overly ornamented—the kind of simple, striking tableware that lets the food shine. Great for gifts.

SIX

Fashion: It Rhymes with Passion

"The only difference between us and other mammals is our ability to accessorize."

—*Steel Magnolias*

"I will never be the woman with the perfect hair who can wear white and not spill on it."

—*Sex and the City*

" 'Sensible' shoes are what your third-grade math teacher wore. No one ever wanted to grow up and look like her."

—Miranda Morrison, co-owner and founder of Sigerson Morrison

"What makes something right is that you wear *it*. It doesn't wear *you*."

—Lida Burpee, advertising executive

Age and experience, I'm happy to say, give a woman the confidence to realize that while she may not have *all* the answers, she at least knows where to look for them. For the most part, I look in my closet. Don't blame me. My fortune cookie read: "Good Clothes Open Many Doors. Go Shopping." Some of us love to shop (make that a capital *L*) finding it incredibly exciting, enriching, rewarding, and fun. Then there are those of us who would be happy if they ordered everything online and never went inside a store again. Which doesn't make them bad people. I know probably three women in the world like this. This advice, verbatim, from my friend Cara: "If you're getting the skirt, get the jacket and blouse too. It will be a nuisance to hunt down coordinating pieces and the outfit will never look coordinated."

Who cares if you have to hunt something down—isn't that the *point* of it? And who cares if it *coordinates*. Aren't "coordinates" something about latitude and longitude? "There's so much out there that exploring and finding is half the fun," says designer Mary Ann Restivo.

The two things I like to do most in the world are eat and shop. And when push comes to shove, I would rather shop than eat. I care deeply about this season's fashion *must-haves,* even if I don't actually feel I must have them. In reality, I mostly wear all black because I live in New York and I never have a thing to wear. I am very big on outlets and truly believe that shopping *is* an outlet. When someone talks about an "important" piece of jewelry, a "fashion-forward" mule, an "essential" beach bag, or a "genius" pair of sunglasses, I snap to attention. You know you are deeply, profoundly into this world when you can understand the concept of loving something *so* much you can't bear to *wear it;* having sheets so luxurious you wouldn't dream of ever sleeping on them. I have a friend who bought a pair of fabulous red satin Jimmy Choos on sale that she is scared to wear for fear of nicking a heel or tarnishing the surface or having them rained on.

But fashion isn't just feelings, it's *knowledge.* You need to know when the Harrods January sale starts, when in July the sales start in Rome, when it's tax-free week in New York, when it's 70 percent off at Bergdorf's and they are *giving* it away. It's also about dreams. I had a wonderful fashion dream the other night where I said to the saleswoman at Barneys: "The size two is swimming on me. Do you have it in a smaller size?" And the way I know I dream in *color* is that I have occasional dreams about sample sales where I've bought the green Nanette Lepore but worry if I should have bought the *pink* Nanette Lepore instead.

There are good shoppers. There are nonshoppers. Then there are the extremes: fashionistas and fashion victims. You know you're a fashionista when you truly believe that window dressing is an art form so you worship Barneys creative director and author Simon Doonan; when you can say "faux pink croc clutch" with a straight face; when you can call something "louche" and mean it; when a color like "plummy sienna" sounds normal; when you have days— even *weeks*—where your life revolves around finding the perfect folding umbrella; when you pass by an upscale dry cleaner and linger on the pretty dresses in the window, forgetting momentarily that they aren't for sale. You know you're a fashion *victim* if you live in New York and pay retail. Or if you really *must* have this season's *must-have*. Or if you don't feel well dressed unless you turn yourself into an Anna Wintour clone.

Everyone who loves fashion has at least one story of triumph. Here's one of mine. A few years ago, at Daffy's, a New York discount boutique, I fell in love with a beautifully classic natural alpaca winter coat that looked a lot like an Armani. Daffy's removes the designer label from the garment, but the price tag on the clothes gives a clue as to its status. The tag on this coat said the price now was $198, marked down from the original price of $2,550. *$2,550!* The price of a used Volkswagen! A week in Paris at the Ritz! I not only bought the coat, I carried that price tag in the pocket of the coat for three winters. Whenever someone said, "what a gorgeous coat," I thanked them and pulled out the tag to show them what made it even prettier.

The nice thing about fashion is that it doesn't always *have* to make sense. (A recent designer collection in Paris featured "evening swimsuits" and a "sleeveless coat.") It just has to make you feel good and hopefully *look* good without ever feeling intimidated by dictates, driven by trends, or excluded by price. It's reassuring to know that even—and especially—the people who make the clothes can sound like they aren't speaking a known language when they talk about fashion. *"J'adoring it!"* says fashion writer Guy Trebay, quoting a stylist at the Paris shows (slightly tongue-in-chic I think). That in itself makes fashion—especially upscale fashion—less intimidating to me.

Stephen MacMillan Moser, writing online in an www .austinchronicle.com article, noted that "Fashion Wire Daily recently ran a few gems of 'Fashionspeak.' They quote Donatella Versace as saying, 'I want people to wear my clothes . . .' And Marc Jacobs saying, 'It's about clothes . . .' and Alexander McQueen saying, 'It was all about the clothes . . .' and James Mischka as saying, 'This collection's about clothes.'

"Excuse me," notes Mr. Moser, "but it should be fairly obvious when you're seeing a clothing designer's collection that it's about the *clothes.*" He goes on to point out another vapid fashion-speak habit: the description of a collection. Donna Karan as quoted in the *San Francisco Examiner*, "There's no day or night, it's transseasonal, ageless. It's about love and passion. There are no rules . . . I am constantly overwhelmed by the natural creativity around me. It just blows me away. Sunsets, sky, earth, rocks. I'm a beach girl . . ." Mr. Moser concludes, "Yeah, me, too, Donna. And I like puppies and Christmas, too, but let's keep it to ourselves."

Beyond the hype, there's hope. And some common sense. As Bernice Kwok-Gabel, formerly the senior press officer for the Metropolitan Museum's Costume Institute and now director of public relations and cultural affairs at Hermès, points out, "The rule today is few rules." There are more choices (like wool and cashmere year-round), more options (shawls and scarves and shrugs and capes), more freedom (no hosiery), more technology (microfiber, woven leather, featherlight shearling, stretch satin), more ways and places to find what you're looking for (when Prada opens an outlet in Italy, you know you're in luck). And it's pretty easy to separate the Wheat from the Chaff (I capped them because they sound suspiciously like two new J. Crew fall colors) and get spot-on fashion advice from people who know what they're talking about. Reading reviews these days can make you laugh out loud, they are so funny and fresh and candid. The reverential tone is gone, and whether it's a fashion force or farce is now duly and juicily noted.

FASHION STATEMENTS

Here's some sage (another color!) advice from a group of six women who talk the talk and walk the walk: New York designer Mary Ann Restivo, who has her own chic accessories line and has dressed everyone, with great style and easy elegance, from opera stars to governors' wives; Paula Faulk, former senior vice president at Giorgio Armani in New York and now general merchandise manager and senior vice president at Ferragamo, who knows what sophisticated women today *want* in their wardrobes; Bernice Kwok-Gabel, who understands all the brilliance and originality of fashion and style with a historical and contemporary perspective;

Christine Celle, the French founder of Calypso (www.calypso-celle.com), brilliantly conceived boutiques that showcase colorful, flirtatious clothes inspired by the French Riviera; Jenny Feldman, trend follower and trendsetting fashion news editor at *Elle* magazine; and Miranda Morrison, co-owner and founder of the Sigerson Morrison shoe empire. Hers are shoes you have to love: pretty, well-made, stylish, nothing too fancy or froufrou—perfect pitch for urban days and evenings.

SHOES

"You know what you look like to me, with your good bag and your cheap shoes? You look like a rube. A well scrubbed, hustling rube with a little taste."

—Dr. Hannibal Lechter to Clarissa in the movie *The Silence of the Lambs*

"Women should buy the best shoes they can afford. They are such a fundamental tool for getting around and forming first impressions—cheap shoes can ruin a great day and a great look. Expensive, all leather-shoes will last better and be more appealing than their crummy counterparts."

—Miranda Morrison

- Ms. Morrison suggests that "assuming you do spring for the good pairs, invest in some shoe trees (wooden are best, but plastic ones from Ikea and Muji are great for traveling) and use them after each wearing. This gives your shoes a double life span, as it puts back the snap and keeps them from resembling sloppily made molds of your foot."

- To the question of whether some styles are always in fashion, Ms. Morrison replies, "Certain shoes never seem to be entirely out of style. Ballerinas, evening sandals, flip-flops, Capri sandals, penny loafers, plain knee-length fitted boots, all seem less subject to the vagaries of fashion than any other classification."

- Jellies sandals melt in Egypt; rope-soled espadrilles get

ruined in the rain; fabric shoes are the only kind that don't stretch; there is no way you'll catch the subway if you're running in retro raffia wedges, but who cares?

- Do not despair—you are not alone: "The art of walking elegantly and with confidence in teetering heels is something only a small percentage of women have as a birthright," Ms. Morrison says. "Wearing them does serve to push out your bosom and your bottom in a way which men find sexy, which is the point after all."

- The nice thing about shoes is that no matter how heffalumpy you might be feeling about your body, you can still fit into and strut around in a pair of sexy, pencil thin, shiny, chic of-the-moment shoes.

- Some shoes are trickier than others and inspire strong opinions. Take the seemingly innocent sandal. Anika Chapin says, "The governing rule on sandals, in my mind, is temperature. Although it may be all right to wear *white* after Labor Day these days, it is *not okay* to wear sandals in the winter, unless you live close to the equator. I cannot fathom why people do this, anyway—sandals aren't that comfortable, let's be honest, and cold feet are always uncomfortable. This also goes for sandals with socks—you aren't fooling anyone. Socks are technically undergarments, and you know why? Because nobody wants to look at them, I promise."

Anika is a woman who also takes on Birkenstocks. "We know, we know, they're so comfortable and of course you can wear them, but only with certain restrictions: not in the winter, not with that ugly strap around the heel, not so beaten up that the sole has stratified into flaky leather levels, and not with socks, *ever*. And keep in mind, if you do wear them, no one will be looking at you going 'cute shoes,' 'cute feet,' or even 'cute legs.' They'll be looking at you thinking, Oh, Birkenstocks. Those must be comfortable."

Nothing is simple. Consider the slingback. Slingbacks can be the perfect pair of shoes for spring—elegant and delicate, yet still with some coverage and protection, yet . . . you can never wear them with pants. First of all, the back hem of your pants will invariably get stuck between your heel and the shoe. Second of all—and this is counterintuitive—the highest-heeled pumps can be easier to walk in than a low-heeled slingback. Without getting too technical, one of the selling points of a slingback—its comfortable flexibility—means that your heel will not stay put. A slingback "walk" tends to be shuffling and awkward.

Ms. Chapin, who (you can probably tell) worked in a shoe store during college breaks, says what amazed her were the women who would come in, see a shoe they liked, and ask "What sizes do you have this in?" "*Why?*" asks Ms. Chapin. "They only need to know if we have it in *their* size. This happened all the time and made us all crazy."

TRENDS

Trends are for women with the thrill-seeking gene. And trends are why God made Target and H&M—if you hate the fun little orange plastic clutch after a week, well, you're only out $12.99. Ms. Kwok-Gabel thinks that "everyone should have fun with fashion" and that's what trends do. If you're feeling playful, or in the mood to go a little out of your comfort zone, or just in a bad mood, cheer yourself up with something trendy. The whole idea of fashion and makeup trends are that they are in one day and out the other—something like faux python or a frilly tank top or aqua shadow don't have a long life span. So enjoy them while they're "in" and "fun." That way you won't find yourself on the back page of *Glamour* as a "Fashion Don't."

A CERTAIN AGE

With age comes wisdom and if you listen to Ms. Restivo, it also comes with a cashmere shawl or ruffled collar. "When you get to be a certain age, you always want to be wearing something that enhances your face—a collar, a scarf, a necklace." Ms. Feldman from *Elle* magazine combines a thought on "age appropriate" with rules vs. no rules.

"Dressing one's age is a meaningless concept. Some of the chicest middle-aged women and older women still dress as they did when they were in their twenties. I think the key to dressing well as you age is being consistent, discovering your personal style, and sticking to that look—whether it's hippie bohemian . . . or classic tailoring. Something that's tarty—i.e., a too-tight jean skirt—will look cheap on an eighteen-year-old, a thirty-year-old, and a sixty-year-old. What's the difference?"

EVERY WOMAN NEEDS

Ms. Restivo, along with every other designer and editor, believes that every woman needs a good tailor. And for Ms. Restivo, high-quality accessories are key.

Ms. Faulk suggests that a really functional wardrobe should include:

- A classic V-neck cashmere.
- A great blazer or jacket that makes you feel like you look elegant and feel stylish.
- A great pair of shoes—what makes them great is up to you. It could be because they are beautiful or because they make you feel good or they're practical. Research, though; find out which manufacturer's last is perfect for you and stay with that.
- A really good handbag—something that's both smart and functional. And finally . . .
- A great pair of dark pants—go for black or charcoal. Ideally, you should be able to wear them at least three seasons. Ms. Faulk, who travels all over the world, says, "If you go on a trip for a week and just take two pairs of pants, you'll be fine. All you have to add are some pearls." She adds, "I know it can be done. When I first started traveling for Armani, I would lug absolutely *everything* and then think, Look at all the money I've wasted from buying all this stuff I really didn't need."

- Along with Ms. Kwok-Gabel and Ms. Restivo, she believes in investing in a great winter coat.

AND DON'T FORGET

- A white shirt. "You can layer them with tanks underneath or with pretty beaded tops under. "Often," Ms. Faulk says, "I put on a white Oxford cloth boys' shirt from Brooks Brothers, go off to work, and feel wonderful in something so simple, crisp, and fresh. Plus, white looks great on everyone in a sea of black."

- A little black dress. Can you say "Audrey Hepburn"? "I think with the little black dress," Ms. Kwok-Gabel says, "the idea has changed. It was really about liberating women originally, but now it's evolved. Now it's just the dress a woman pulls out and feels confident in, knowing that it looks just right and appeals to the opposite sex. These days, it doesn't even have to be black." Ms. Feldman concurs: "It's something you can take from work to cocktails. What's more timeless than that?"

- Finally: When it comes to what you should buy, Ms. Restivo wisely says, "Start with need. The rest is easy."

EVENING DRESSING

My idea of transitioning from day into evening is to unbutton one button and revive my mascara in the cab on the way. But for a real evening look, Ms. Restivo says, "When I go out at night, I want there to be a different attitude—something special. So even if it's just putting on a pair of earrings or pulling my hair back, it changes the way I look and feel."

Asked if there is a difference between those of us who *read W* and those of us who actually *buy* the hand-beaded chiffon ballgown in the pages, Ms. Restivo says there is. "Rich women believe in color. They can afford to. They don't wear a lot of black. They don't need their clothes to be so serviceable. And only rich women wear white coats."

FASHION PHILOSOPHY

Asked how a woman knows what's right for her, Christiane Celle of Calypso says, "In general, we have two kinds of customers walk into our stores. Some know *exactly* what they want. The others have *no* idea and leave it to the salesperson to help. Our store rule is that a saleswoman cannot let a customer leave with something that's wrong for them; that isn't flattering or becoming." My friend Harriet looks at this from a customer's point of view and says: "If a salesperson tells you *everything* looks good on you, thank her for her help but tell her you prefer to make your own decisions."

When it *does* look good, everyone benefits. "Men call and say thank you," Ms. Celle adds. "One man said, 'My wife just bought a lilac outfit at your store. I love it! She usually only wears black.'" She points out that from her in-store observations, there are so many women who say, "Oh, I can't wear beige." Or "I can't wear a square neckline" when they're just not adventurous or willing to try something new. Mary Ann Restivo says she is used to hearing her customers say something like, "I'm too short to wear a longer jacket" and suggests "It's really all about stance and attitude. If you act tall, you'll *look* taller."

Ms. Celle suggests that if you are not completely confident of your look, you should go to a store you can trust to give you honest and helpful advice; take as much time as you need to try different things and not feel rushed; establish a relationship with the salesperson and don't leave until you're sure you've gotten just the right thing. Ms. Faulk believes that women today are more style-conscious and smarter than ever. But her advice is, "If you don't feel like you have your own natural style or creativity, just keep it simple and you'll always look great."

And from Ms. Feldman, "I think looking great is about an attitude, a certain confidence . . . The right woman can always pull off an unbecoming or kooky concept. That said, I will always appreciate clothes that are flattering and easy to wear. American designers are particularly adept at giving us this."

Does It Feel Good? Does It Look Good? Can I Walk in It? Do I Care?

Ms. Celle knows that American women want to dress comfortably. "American women love materials that they know are comfortable to wear—cashmere, silk, cotton." Asked if French women have the same desire, she laughs. "France, no! They just want to look sexy and beautiful!"

"Italians," says Ms. Faulk, who works for an Italian company, "are more body conscious and more confident. They think about what to buy and how they're going to wear it. They know what to invest in. They're more aware of tailoring and having it 'just so.' They have everything fitted." (One more vote for a good tailor.)

But here's a vote for how to be gorgeous and sensible at the same time, from Ms. Restivo: "The newest and easiest way to dress is to keep the same basics underneath, then just accessorize your look in different ways. These days, there are wonderful jackets, scarves, shawls, shrugs, sweaters in fabrics from cashmere to taffeta. And part of what makes it so easy is that things don't have to be so matched anymore."

Very Few Rules, but a Lot of Common Sense

Black and blue, sure. Black and brown, great. Leggings under skirts and dresses, good to go. White jeans after Labor Day? Ms. Feldman's philosophy: "Breaking sartorial rules is the epitome of cool—and it always will be." What about the few prohibitions that may still exist—like not wearing black at weddings or not wearing flip-flops to the White House? Ms. Kwok-Gabel says, "I think women are smarter about it. You have to notice your environment. Rules still apply if you keep respect in mind. For the wedding question, I think you have to be considerate of religion and respectful of where you are. If you have a great black dress, but the wedding is going to be sixty percent people of an older generation, then maybe save it for the wedding when you know that most of the people there will be younger. It's really a matter of common sense."

Capris and Other Cropped Pants

Capris can be an elegant classic and can hide a multitude of sins if worn with an untucked white button-down shirt. However, it's important to remember that they can also be incredibly unflattering. In the immortal words of Anika Chapin's manager when Anika waitressed at the Comfort Diner, "The shorter the pants, the bigger the ass."

Jeans

Okay, no one thinks a woman of a certain age does herself a favor by wearing "granny" jeans. You know, the baggy ones that aren't really the right size or cut. "Jeans," says designer Mary Ann Restivo, "are universal. But they are not universally appropriate." And she points out that it is very hard to be honest with a woman about how she looks in jeans because very few women *don't* think they look good in them. Jeans are so ubiquitous that, Ms. Restivo adds, "Today, if a store owner or designer wants to sell a sweater or jacket or camisole and convince a customer that it's a great piece for her, all you have to do is say 'And you can wear it with jeans.' " Ms. Celle says, "I will always wear jeans. But when you are my age, forty-seven, with two children, I'm more comfortable wearing them as classics with flat shoes, *not* cut low and *not* with high heels." She correctly says that these days, there are so many different kinds of jeans that you can always find a pair that's flattering for your body and for your age.

All About Jeans: Fit, Fashion, and Who Isn't Fanatical?

"It's all about a girl and her rear view," says Kim France, the editor of the Condé Nast shopping magazine *Lucky*. "How many different ways can you make the rear view look good?" "Jeans are an emotional purchase," says Robert Burke, the fashion director of Bergdorf Goodman. "They have the most sex appeal of any garment you'll buy." He adds what we all know: that the idea of jeans with sex appeal now appeals to men *and* women along with all age groups. Cuts, fabrics, hip heights, styles, studs, washes, weave, hems, stitching, waistlines, fading, and brand names *all* matter.

As far as getting the *right* fit, Jenny Feldman of *Elle* says bring a friend with you. And if you are going to be wearing jeans with a particular kind of shoe—flats or heels—bring the shoes with you. Ms. Feldman counsels that all jeans stretch, so don't get too big a size. But too tight," she says, "is never cute unless you're Kate Moss." She also believes that the idea of "perfect fit" is hard to pin down since jeans are so trendy that "perfect fit" is kind of a moving target.

Eleanor Ylvisaker, an executive at Earnest Sewn jeans, says, "There are different fits that look good on different body types, but no matter what the cut of the jean is, it looks best when the back rise is high enough to cover the seat, and the front rise remains low and sexy. The inseam should touch the ground when the wearer is standing on her toes so that it maintains that nice break, no matter what shoes are paired with the jeans." But lest you think that Ms. Ylvisaker is the Eva Braun of denim, she adds, "The most important part of a good jean fit is that the wearer feels both comfortable and confident in them."

FASHION MISTAKES

"Showing too much flesh," all the fashion pros agree. Especially when you are older than, say, fifteen. "A cropped top doesn't look good on *anyone*," says Ms. Kwok-Gabel. "A woman after a certain age has a wonderful wisdom and maturity she exudes, along with her own personal aesthetic. Of course, she could wear a little plaid skirt and pigtails, but why would she *want* to?"

More mistakes: short shorts on anyone, especially older women. Bike shorts. Really long hair on older women. Jeans at the opera. Women of a certain age with lots of visible tattoos. Huge, obviously fake boobs. Over-the-top *Sopranos* jewelry. And back to jeans: "When jeans are cut too low," says Eleanor Ylvisaker, "and your shirt doesn't touch the top of the jean, there is the danger of a tacky look—especially if the waistband is too tight and it creates rolls over the top of the jean." Forget "mistake"—we're talking "nightmare" here.

WHAT MAKES FASHION FUN?

Ms. Faulk says, "Women are emotional. We all love to be stimulated by choices, by what's new. And we all love a sense of discovery. And color," she says, "adds spark. I travel with ten or twelve different scarves—all different, all bright colors—to accent my basics." And to me, impulse things should be fun. Anything white that's only going to last a season, for example. Something whimsical. Like a pair of espadrilles. Why not?"

I think what makes fashion fun is seeing what Björk is wearing. Not to be mean, but fashion is fun when it's a huge mistake, like the time Lara Flynn Boyle wore what looked like a tutu at the Academy Awards. Fashion is fun when someone like the Olsen twins start wearing ratty, tatty clothes and start a huge trend. Fashion is fun when a heavy-hitter Italian designer acknowledges getting some of the ideas for his new collection from bike messenger outfits.

Fashion is *not fun* when it's too safe: now just about every woman at every awards show has a stylist so it's all about being tasteful and ladylike. Fashion is not fun when you wear the clothes exactly the way the store has put them together and don't use any imagination. Twin sets are a great example: you can't just wear a plain twin set with a skirt to your knees. *Boring.* You need to *do* something with it—like a riff on retro or a whole bunch of colorful crocheted necklaces.

Sample sales, especially the ones held by a big-deal designer, can be total fun if:

- You're there on the first day.
- You wear a model's shoe size (9–11) because the shoes (gently worn) from the shows are for sale.
- You are a model's size (2–4) because you might find a fabulous one-of-a-kind piece made just for the shows.

Bring cash—the line is shorter. And it's a good idea to wear something form-fitting, like a tank top, so you can try things on without having to go to the dressing room.

Lingerie

Always clean; never frayed. Fancy, sexy, silky, shiny, or simply Banana Republic. For classic, well-cut, top-quality you can't beat Hanro for anything from camisoles to T-shirts. And not to digress, but have you noticed that only men call them "panties"? Women—at least everyone I know—calls them "underpants."

Good bras

The pretty ones, like Wacoal and Chantelle and "preferably," says my friend Harriet, "a bit sexy. And sturdy jogging bras. I can't tell you how often I have seen women running in the park (usually amply endowed) with their boobs bouncing. First of all, it looks just *awful*—how can you be doing the right thing for your health and at the same time be so oblivious to not giving your breasts the proper support? And it's not a money issue. Good jogging bras can come from the Gap or Kmart, not just from expensive running stores."

A decidedly French POV comes from executive lingerie fitter Pauline Rueda who works at New York's BraSmyth boutique. Ms. Rueda says a woman's complete bra wardrobe needs to consist only of an everyday bra (with no cup seams) to be worn under a sweater or shirt and a strapless bra for evening. The everyday bra can be simple or lacy, but, as Ms. Rueda says, "It should be beautiful and feel wonderful. That's what changes the attitude and makes a woman feel good." Ms. Rueda swears the French do it best: hard to argue with that when she points out that undergarment experts go to specialty design schools for approximately five years before they graduate. Asked about the simple cotton bras from the Gap that are so popular? A very French shrug and a dismissive "for teenagers."

Swimwear

"Everyone who is young should understand that every minute they spend *not* wearing a bikini is a complete and utter waste."

—Nora Ephron

- Here's to Malia Mills, a woman who not only sells great-looking bathing suits but who realized way before most people that your top might be an 8 and your bottom might be a 12. That's because we're humans. And so Ms. Mills decided to start selling two-piece suits separately. Ms. Mills says women come into her Manhattan swimwear shops (www.maliamills.com) "all day long with a checklist of what works for their body" and she wants to tell them to throw it all away. "Certain tips may be helpful," she says. "But for me, it's about what I call the Pamela Anderson effect. Whatever critics say about her style, there's no denying that Pamela Anderson feels great in the clothes she wears."

- Jenny Feldman says that "J. Crew is every young woman's friend when it comes to bathing suit shopping. Most of us aren't the same size on top and bottom, and they sell pieces separately. Plus, they make every color, style, and pattern you could want, and you can try on and then return in the privacy of your own apartment if your choice doesn't work out. Not to mention, for a wallet-friendly price of $80 or so, who can complain?"

- I have friends who swear by Kmart's selection and amazingly low prices.

- Lands' End has one of the most complete selections of swimwear, for any kind of taste and any kind of body. And this is a company that seems to feel our pain—they have an "Anxiety Zones" online (click on Swim). If you want to know which suits will help you any specific problem, from defining your waist to deemphasizing your hips, they'll give you specific solutions. And if you're *really* anxious, you can call and speak to a Lands' End Specialty Shopper who can walk you through it.

- The Complaint Department: Oh, why do stores (especially department stores) still insist on cramming bathing suits together so tightly that you need to use brute force to extricate one to look at it? Where do the companies who make suits find those hideous tropical hibiscus leaf prints they still use and those scratchy, shiny, ugly fabrics? And do they really think we want to wear shocking pink with navy blue or bright orange? Why does a store carry five hundred styles of little bikinis and five styles of suits suitable for the post-tween set? Why are lights in the dressing rooms so bright that you could do a lobotomy in there? Why, to look at yourself in the suit, do you usually have to *leave* the dressing room area and go out into the public areas to humiliate yourself by looking (and having others look) at yourself in a gigantic and unflattering three-way mirror? And why did that evil salesgirl suggest "something with a little skirt or coverup" to me? A few suggestions: softer lights; flattering three-way mirrors; pretty dressing rooms; a salesperson who knows the stock and is happy to help you edit and select; a beautifully chosen selection rather than thousands of suits; a fitter who could advise you right on the spot and help with any alterations; a glass of chilled champagne to take the edge off the experience.

Jewelry

Well, here's an area where everyone has a different opinion. I think just go with your own taste and sensibility and find a jeweler you trust. Ms. Restivo, for example, believes that "once you're in your forties or fifties, it's better to get a major piece than a bunch of meaningless little ones. A good ring—diamonds or sapphires, for instance. Or a great necklace." She is a proponent of pieces that can be worn again and again—especially for women who have their own well-established look.

On the other hand, there is Lindsay Cain, creator of the store Femmegems (www.femmegems.com) and who speaks for a younger woman. "Keep jewelry pretty," Ms. Cain says. "Be less concerned about provenance and price and more focused on being creative and having fun. Don't," she cautions, "get locked into thinking you need to be wearing your grandma's jewelry—you can wear something real or you can get it at a flea market and mix it up." She adds, "If you can get a piece that makes you feel special, it doesn't have to be expensive." Rules? "None," says Ms. Cain. "You can make yourself sparkle at any age." But, she adds "Never a big necklace *and* big earrings—do one or the other. The only exception to that is if you're wearing jewelry to a big-deal black-tie event."

Pearls . . .

Old-fashioned or au courant? Real or faux? "Pearls are a great staple. They've evolved," Ms. Cain says. "They're no longer so formal and ladylike. And there are different types. I like seed pearls for a younger, sweeter, preppier look. Freshwater pearls for everyone. Vintage pearls to layer and mix." Can you tell if they're real or not? Ms. Cain points out that real pearls are gritty, but helpfully adds, "No one is going to take a nibble on your pearls at a dinner party!" *Real* pearls are not so simple. Like any other piece of serious jewelry, they're an investment. To judge their quality, you need to know about color, luster, orient, shape, size, and things like staggered layers of nacre crystals. Or you need a good jeweler to explain it to you and guide you.

. . . and Diamonds

Tiffany takes jewelry seriously. They even put out a sweetly elegant and informative little book for the betrothed and befuddled about buying a Tiffany diamond. It includes everything from the "4Cs"—cut, clarity, color, and carat weight—to the flaws and imperfections that Tiffany won't tolerate. Which include everything from "misshapen facets" to "a wavy girdle to abrasions and a subadamantine luster." Who knew?

Sigmund Freud asked, "What does a woman want, dear God, what does she want?"

WELL, IN ADDITION TO NEEDING THAT GOOD TAILOR, YOU'LL WANT:

- A good hairdresser
- A good hair colorist (someone who doesn't take hours and hours—I know it's an art, but they're not painting the Sistine Chapel)
- A good manicurist and pedicurist (someone who will try

their best to squeeze you in even when they're totally booked)

- A good masseuse, even if you don't go that often. If you travel a lot for business, collect names of top people in different cities or countries. *Allure* magazine is good about listing spas and salons across the country.

- A store where you know someone who is a personal shopper or has great style—or a salesperson who will call you when things are going on sale

- A dry cleaner who won't shrink your cashmere sweater or lose your black jeans. A dry cleaner who can hem something for you in a day.

- The name and number of a personal trainer and a nutritionist, even if you never get around to going to either

- The name of a makeup artist. You might never use him or her, but just in case you're going someplace fabulous, you'll have someone who can glam you up.

- The name and number of a jeweler who can fix things and appraise things. Someone who isn't with a store and who has his or her own business is best.

These days most women will share *everything*—the names of all good resources with a few exceptions. Because a good, reliable cleaning woman is so hard to find, women are loathe to share the secret of their sparkling house. Also, if you think a friend wants to turn into a mini-you, which is creepy, hey, get *your* own ash blond and colorist! And professionally, no one can share her shrink since for most psychotherapists and psychiatrists this both is a potential conflict and a blurring of boundaries. Be a little wary of a shrink who *will* see your friends or family members.

ALL YOU NEED TO KNOW ABOUT STYLE AND FASHION

1. Even if you wear the clothes you bought in Paris and the shoes you bought in Paris the very same day you bought them in Paris, you won't look French to the French.

2. One of the worst crimes in America is overaccessorizing. Try to remember Coco Chanel's suggestion for how you know you've got it right: after you're dressed, look in the mirror and take one thing off.

3. Never wear a "jogging suit," not even to jog. *Especially* not to jog.

4. Woolite kills bras—wash them in shampoo.

5. If you're going to *have* a baby, don't wear anything that makes *you* look like the baby: no eyelet, no bows, no baby-doll styles, no pastels, no rickrack, no baby blue or pink.

6. The coolest designers tend to be the ones whose names you can't pronounce and forget about spelling them correctly: Azzedine Alaia, Junya Watanabe, Heidi Slimane, Jean-Charles de Castlebajac, Rei Kawakubo. It *is* helpful to know how to pronounce these names if you are going to shop in a snooty place that sells their clothes.

7. Never "fake," always "faux." It just sounds better.

8. Never say "garmento" unless you work in the garment center.

9. Shopping for women's clothes if you're bigger than a size 2 is hard in Asia. When I was shopping in Hong Kong the only things that fit me were shoes and pearls and jade and anything made to order. Even though the always-petite saleswomen were excruciatingly polite, they made a little face when I went to reach for a cashmere sweater on the shelf, since even the largest was like a size for My Big Fat Barbie.

10. "Sample sales can be great," says Ms. Restivo, "but don't buy something just because it is so well priced." "You must truly love it," adds my friend Dominique Bigar Khan.

AND FINALLY, *WHY?*

- Sweaters with three-quarter sleeves and short-sleeved cashmere sweaters. Barbara Harrison logically says, "It's either cold or it's hot. Either you need your arms or legs covered or you don't."

- Flip-flops. Snow. *No.*

- "Matchy-matchy," as fashion editors call it. As far as I can tell from my extensive royalty watching, only Queen Elizabeth still puts it all together in quite such a determinedly building-block way. Camilla comes close.

- High high heels

- The thong

- Implants

- Bathing suits you can't actually *swim* in. The ones decorated with jewels so weighty that you would sink instantly. The ones with little tiny bra tops and miniscule bottoms that are meant for parading, that show off your breasts, not your breaststroke.

- Snow boots you can't actually wear in the snow

- "Pashima" and "cashmere" you buy on the street. First of all, they're acrylic or worse. The $25 black "pashmina" shawl my friend Marsha bought wasn't colorfast and started to bleed the black onto her skin during a long opera in a warm auditorium.

- Confusing dictates. A friend's daughter, who had just started a job at a major consulting firm, was told that the following Friday was "dress-down casual day." Pants? T-shirt? Loafers? She didn't have any idea what that meant. For men, it always seems to mean Dockers and button-down shirts.

- Backpacks. Yes, they are better for your back than a shoulder bag. But a backpack is a style sacrifice—the best you can hope for is that it is inoffensive. If you must, the small Longchamps ones come in cool colors, fit a city wardrobe, and don't make you look like you're off to backpack through the Alps.

- Legwarmers

CELEBRITY FASHION

Celebrity! Yes, it could happen to *you* and you need to be ready. What does being in the public eye demand of you? Do you want it? Will you be up to it? Caroline Schaefer, former senior editor at *Us Weekly,* answers some of the most pressing questions.

What can celebrities do that mere mortals can't? Ms. Schaefer says, "You can get away with sending things back; demanding that everything is perfect (your *own* description of "perfect," of course); you can show up hours late; abuse people physically and emotionally; insist on only green M&Ms; throw things; get free stuff. (For a list of strange backstage demands, go to www.thesmokinggun.com.)

If the glare of the spotlight bothers you, Ms. Schaefer suggests: "If you want the paparazzi to leave you alone, wear the same outfit you've worn before. Jennifer Aniston, for example, does that on purpose. She doesn't go out that much and when she does she'll wear something she's already been photographed in."

Do you have to look nice all the time? "Yes," Ms. Schaefer says. "Except if you're Michael Moore or Courtney Love. Real stars—think Catherine Zeta-Jones and JLo—are always well groomed and beautifully turned out. Their clothes and shoes and bags are by designers who lavish gorgeous goodies on them, they have an entourage of hairdressers and makeup artists and stylists, they *command* attention."

Oprah says, "It takes a village to get ready, between the hair, the makeup, and the clothes."

INTERNATIONAL FASHION AT YOUR FINGERTIPS

www.antipodium.com: Aussie designs—beyond the expected, beachwear and accessories with fresh style and unexpected styles.

www.belmacz.com: English jewelry—precious and semi-precious—by a young designer featured in British *Vogue*.

www.netaporter.com: The mother ship. Everything—trend reports to the latest designers to a beauty magazine to what's on the runway. Along with "what to buy" comes advice about what to pair it with. Jewelry, accessories, evening wear, day wear, shoes, bags—the most complete and totally seductive site. Very chic and very cher; from Jimmy Choo to Miu Miu. Mercifully, there is a Sale section. Because it's an English site, prices are in pounds and dollars.

www.deroemer.com: Not the same old, same old. This English site is the place to find luxe cashmere sweaters and Indian-inspired jewelry. The designer, Tasmin deRoemer, used to work with Jade Jagger.

www.chicshoppingparis.com: New York isn't enough for you? Francophile? Love to shop in France? Stay current with this up-to-the-moment guide to what's going on in Paris. Written, of course, by two Americans!

READ ALL ABOUT IT

www.dailycandy.com: Must-read. The current fashion bible/arbiter/everyday news and reviews on everything stylish. What's hot and what's not. Travel, food, fashion, and lots of plugs and links for products. Great on up-coming sample sales in NY and LA. Everyone reads it. There are national and city-specific locations.

soifferhaskin.com: This is the New York husband/wife team who holds the best and biggest sales—from Loro Piana to Max Mara on West 33rd Street. Get on their mailing list, on-line or via mail.

The best book: *Love, Loss, and What I Wore* by Ilene Beckerman. A little charmer that's turned into a classic. It's Ms. Beckerman's personal take on how much of our lives, our moods, and our memories connect directly to our choice of wardrobe.

SEVEN

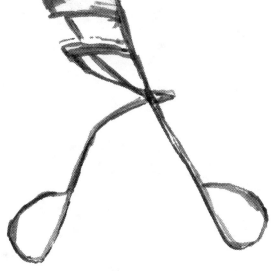

Get in Touch with Your Outer Self:
All for Beauty

"I only use Crème de La Mer moisturizing cream. I have no idea if it works, but I always wonder how much worse I'd look if I didn't use it."

—John Waters, director of *Pink Flamingo* and *Hairspray*

"I did the best I could with everything God gave me. If I did those horrible things, I wouldn't look this good physically."

—Imelda Marcos

"Every sidewalk is a runway."

—Ad for company selling hair products, seen on a New York taxi

"Thirty-five percent of American women would rather have a good hair day every day than have great sex for the rest of their lives."

—From a study by British hairdresser Charles Worthington

It used to be that the world was divided between *inner* beauty—think Mother Teresa and Joan of Arc and Marie Curie—and *outer* beauty. *Outer* beauty lends itself less to the enrichment of say, saving a country, and more to the enrichment you get from a Clinique body lotion or the miracle you create with a Wonderbra. These days, there is less disconnect between the two. Health and beauty, appearances and feelings coexist, well . . . beautifully.

Beauty and fashion writer Alexandra Marshall discusses the extremes of this, describing Los Angeles salons that are now applying feng shui principles to haircuts. She notes that the beauty industry today "has already appropriated aromatherapy and Ayurveda. These treatments have traditionally served well-being, not style, but in an era when we're more encouraged than ever to express our deepest selves through our looks, there no longer seems to be a disconnect between our appearance and who we really are."

Inner beauty, outer beauty—isn't it really just about feeling happy and content? For many years, I wrote ads and television commercials for Esteé Lauder. And so many of my friends said to me, "Oh, you probably know enough now not to believe any of the hype about lotions and potions. They don't do a thing." On the contrary. I wound up loving the vastness, gorgeousness, and possibilities of it all—the advanced skin care products and technology; the hundreds of global cosmetic brands and products; the fragrances; the treatments; the French names; the exquisite Japanese packaging. What could be more pleasurable than wandering around Bloomingdale's sampling, spritzing, blending, dabbing, applying, lining, blushing, and brushing? Do I believe *everything* the cosmetic companies tell us? No. Do I love being seduced by a bronzing powder, by a soft plum blush, by a delicately scented votive candle? Yes, of course. I do.

Frankly, after a tough day at the office, the business trip from hell, or the week you caught the flu from your child, the best and most effective mood-altering substance you can buy is likely to be a hot pink lipstick, a box of bitter orange and cinnamon Agraria potpourri, a nourishing body wash.

But there is love and there is obsession. And I don't mean the fragrance. Go online to a site like www.makeupalley.com and you will understand what I mean. You know how you might think Gee, this is a good mascara. I really like it. On makeupalley's site, here's a small part of a typical encyclopedic response to the purchase of an inexpensive mascara: "Pinch me, because I think I have died and gone to MASCARA HEAVEN! This stuff is AMAZING, an UBER-MASCARA, an eyelash revolution in a bottle. Everything else pales in comparison." And then the writer helpfully adds her POV about *evening* use of mascara: "At night for more drama, I just add a top coat of L'Oréal Voluminous and *wow*, porno-slut eyelash city." I'd hate to hear this mascara fan and her friends take on "matte" vs. "gloss." And to think that some women are happy with Cetaphil.

Somewhere in between there are women who carefully select what's best for them from what's out there and who take the time to look fabulous. They know the skin care products that work best for them; what shades are most flattering; whose moisturizers are too greasy for them; which foundations are too thick. Do they play the field? Sure. There's always something tempting and yummy at the cosmetic counter.

On a cautionary note, while there is nothing as uplifting as a free ten-minute makeup session at a user-friendly cosmetics counter, there is little as demoralizing as someone in the business who is clueless/insensitive/mildly sadistic. From the highly recommended female dermatologist who was meticulously examining Phoebe's mildly broken-out adolescent skin with a magnifying mirror: *"Perfection,"* this doctor blurted out as she momentarily looked up from her examination. *"Nothing more. Nothing less,"* she added matter-of-factly. Phoebe was terrified. I was horrified. We never went back.

But assuming you will be wearing some makeup, using some skin care products, and picking a dermatologist, how do you know who and what to choose? For a dermatologist, I would suggest setting up consultations with a few and deciding on the basis that you want someone who is medically thorough (does he or she give you whole-body checks for moles and precancer?), gives you sensible proactive advice about your skin, suggests the best anti-sun and anti-aging products for your particular skin, and understands the latest beauty advances and techniques. If you get someone who is a big name and in all the magazines, you run the risk of having fly-by appointments with someone who is much more interested in a celebrity clientele.

When it comes to products, the fact is that there are not only thousands of choices out there but new (*New! Revolutionary! State-of-the-Art!*) products always coming on the market, and just about everything is touted as the next greatest thing. Read *Allure*, read *InStyle* and *Vogue* and *W*, try makeup on when you're at the store, go on some beauty websites, get samples, get professional advice—sift through and you'll start to make sense of it. See who is using what at your gym and ask them. My friend Harriet was in the locker room one winter day and applying a hand cream she recently discovered and now swears by: Neutrogena Norwegian Formula, scented or non, two ounces for about $5. Now everyone at her health club is using it.

Everything in life—from physics to fly-fishing—seems to have a principle to go with it and a philosophy behind it. Why shouldn't an eyelash curler have one too? Katrina Borgstrom, a New York makeup artist who works on editorial and television commercials in addition to doing makeup for special events, has a nicely reassuring one: "What I have learned is that less is more. Don't fuss too much with yourself. Women are beautiful, and the best advice I can give is that happiness does more for your skin than any product can."

That being said, after years of experience, the following are the products this expert swears by:

- Jojoba oil to keep your lashes, brows, and hair conditioned
- Tweezerman tweezers
- Shu Uemura eyelash curler
- Nonpetroleum lip balm (look for it in health food stores)
- Nars Orgasm blush (Katrina says it adds perfect color and glow to any skin)
- Laura Mercier concealer

THEN ALL YOU NEED TO DO . . .
FOUR BASIC STEPS FROM MS. BORGSTROM

1. Make sure your eyebrows are shaped and groomed. Brows are the frame of the face and the most important part.

2. Use a lash curler. If you use this one thing with two coats of good mascara (Lancôme or Dior are favorites), you can totally transform your face.

3. Concealer where you need it and blush to brighten the face.

4. Add a soft berry gloss (for cool skin tones) or a warm, peachy gloss (for warm skin tones).

HEAVY-HITTER LUXURY PRODUCTS VS. DRUGSTORE

Ms. Borgstrom says: "I like to tell women to look at their skin care routine in a similar way they look at their wardrobe. There are some things you buy that are inexpensive and you wear more frequently. And then there are some things you buy that are more luxurious that you use less often but with greater care and attention. Perhaps the reason to go with a more expensive brand is that it makes us feel like we are adding an element of luxury—and that, by itself, is more likely to get us to take better care of our skin!"

DRUGSTORE BEAUTY

- Cetaphil
- Carmex lip moisturizer
- Jergens Natural Glow Daily Moisturizer
- Maybelline Great Lash Mascara
- Vaseline (goes from a lip gloss to a makeup remover to the ultimate cold weather moisturizer)

HIGH/LOW HAIR CARE

Fabulous products for fabulous hair and their high-achieving, low-budget counterparts. From Patrick Melville, owner and creative director of the Warren-Tricomi Salon, Rockefeller Center.

Luxe	Basic
Kérastase Bain Mirroir Shampoo	Pantene Pro V
Kérastase Masquintense	Nexxus Humectress
Redken Rough Paste	Garnier Fructis Surf Wax
Kérastase Volum-Activ	VO5 Volumizer
Redken Water Wax	Murray's Pomade
Kiehl's Silk Groom	Grassroots Styling Cream
Elnett Hairspray	VO5 Quick Hold

CONTACT LENSES: THE SOLUTION

From Anika Chapin: "Color contacts almost always look weird, especially if you have dark eyes and are trying to make them lighter. They all seem to have those small dots on them, which are an instant giveaway that you are wearing contacts. Besides, no one has violet eyes except for Elizabeth Taylor."

From www.ehow.com (a girl can never get too much practical advice): If you have dropped a contact on the floor and can't find it, here's a little trick. Put the leg of a pair of nylons over a vacuum hose and secure it with a rubber band. Turn the vacuum on and run it over the area where the contact could have fallen, keeping the hose about an inch above the floor. Of course, if you are really nearsighted, you'll be on your hands and knees doing this procedure.

GIFT WITH PURCHASE AND PURCHASE WITH PURCHASE

Some women haunt their favorite department stores just waiting to pounce when the seasonal or semiannual Gift with Purchase from large companies like Lauder, Clinique, and Lancôme is available. If you give away your little toilet kit filled with sample sizes, everyone will know where you got it, so it's bad form to regift. But Gift with Purchase is a great way to try new products or products that are new to you without making a major commitment. The best deal and biggest deals can be the holiday gifts that are a purchase with purchase: like a makeup kit with over one hundred brushes, blushes, shadows, and shades that can cost you under $20. And if you are about to replace your Clinique powder anyway, you might as well wait until you can get some extra goodies at the same time. Which brings up the next topic:

Samples and How to Get Them

From Barry Williams, a Bloomingdale's Bobbi Brown makeup consultant for seven years: "You just ask for them. A lot of companies now do mailers, too—they send you a card if you're a customer, and you redeem it for a sample lipstick or something. But mostly, all you have to do is ask."

Really? What about sample hounds? How can you tell if someone is one? Mr. Williams says, "You can recognize them from season to season. Or you watch someone go from counter to counter and then come to you. I don't mind, though, because I figure even if they don't pay for products, someone might see it on them and then buy it. So I give them the samples."

And some premium lines are more liberal with samples than others. Kiehl's, for example, is known for their generosity. Perfumer Bond gives away what look like shiny little bonbons, really just samples of some of their many fragrances. Really, really expensive products like Lauder's Crème de La Mer practically have armed guards near them at the counter.

COSMETIC, SKIN CARE, AND HAIR HIGHLIGHTS

- There is no other aspect of fashion that inspires more uninspired, recycled prose than the beauty arena. If there's a piece on gold eyeshadow, you can count on it being titled something like "Strike Gold!" or "The New Gold Standard!" A new clear gloss will be breathlessly described as "Sheer Magic!" or "Clearly Fabulous!" Many exclamation points (!!!!!) come along for the ride.

- Most women find it easier to be faithful to a husband or lover than to their shampoo or conditioner.

- While you might get some makeup applied free of charge, there is no such thing as a *free beauty makeover.* You will somehow wind up buying hundreds of dollars' worth of product either because you have turned into a true believer once you see your new look or because you feel obligated to buy something. *Are you obligated?* Ms. Borgstrom says, "Yes, they are looking to sell products. However, sometimes you can come across an in-store makeup artist who might want to help with a makeover or an application lesson, but it is customary to buy *something* if you are getting made up."

- There is nothing, absolutely *nothing,* you're currently doing, using, or applying that will *not* make a cosmetic expert or facialist wrinkle her face in disbelief or disappointment. You'll hear things like, "Blue really isn't in the color palette *I* would choose for your eyes," or "You're not using a moisturizer with an SPF in it for sleeping, are you?"

- The Zen of makeup is to spend hundreds of dollars on products to make it look like you're not wearing any makeup at all.

- Cellulite is hereditary. Blame it on your mother. And although there are a lot of products that promise to treat or correct it, this from New York cosmetic-dermatologic surgeon Howard Sobel, MD, in *Harper's Bazaar:* "Nothing can make cellulite disappear completely, although certain ingredients will help it look better temporarily."

- A terrific natural look for any woman is to take a little dab of moisturizer and a little dab of liquid foundation. Mix them together in the palm of your hand, then lightly apply to your face.

- Start accepting your hair fate.

- Get a trim every six to eight weeks even if you're growing your hair out. Unhealthy ends kill the entire hairstyle.

- If you're talking about fragrance with someone in the business, you refer to the actual fragrance as the "juice."

- None of us, even if we took French for years, is sure that we're saying "L'Occitane" correctly.

- A lipstick shade that looks good on everyone and that everyone has used at one point: Black Honey by Clinique. There are fans of Black Honey and there are fanatics. "If Clinique ever discontinues this color, you may see me on a building top on your local six o'clock news."

- Spritzing your face with a mineral water like Evian or Shu Uemura will do nothing to hydrate it unless you immediately follow it up by applying moisturizer.

- *"La beauté n'est pas raisonnable."* Beauty is beyond reason. I'll say. Oddly, this isn't a beauty company slogan but the official slogan of the legendary French design company Baccarat. The sentiment is a little sad but seems less hopeless when it's in French.

SPLIT ENDS: BREAKING UP WITH YOUR HAIRDRESSER

You think it's scary to break up with a boyfriend or a business partner? For most of us, those breakups are a lot easier than leaving your hairdresser or colorist. After all, you probably *like* them. And what if someone else gives you a terrible shag cut or some brassy blond highlights? Don't panic. Hairstylist Carrie Butterworth, from New York's Warren-Tricomi Salon, says, "Hairstylists will take it very well if you try someone else and come back to them. Except for diva stylists, they know they are part of a service industry—their job isn't to make you feel like you did a bad thing, and they will even tell you in a nice way how to change the haircut you're now sorry you've got." Ms. Butterworth points out that, after all, the stylist is usually pleased you came back.

Asked about whether stylists hate it when you rip a picture out of a magazine and say, "This is what I want," Ms. Butterworth says that, on the contrary, most hairdressers are happy to work from a picture, whether it's for a cut or a specific color. But she adds that a superstar colorist at the salon had a client who brought in a picture to show him the shade she wanted—only the picture was black and white.

"THE NEW OLD YOU!!!"

We all know that forty is the new sixty or whatever and that you're only as old as you feel, et cetera, et cetera. But as peppy as it may sound in those upbeat articles in *O*, for everything there is a season. And there is a season for Botox and Restylane. You absolutely know you're ready for plastic surgery when you tell ten people that you're about to turn fifty and not one of them says, "Oh, really, you don't look it." What treatments or steps to take? My friend, Ellen, a beauty editor, says, "I think a woman should do what gives her confidence."

Beauty and Skin Advice by Age
From Katrina Borgstrom:

- "In your *twenties*, no matter how late you've been out, re-move your makeup with a good remover for heavier eye makeup and a good cleanser. Then a light moisturizer. (This is very important!)

- "In your *thirties*, hormonal fluctuations can change skin." Ms. Borgstrom recommends an occasional alpha hydroxy treatment to help brighten the skin and suggests, "introduce eye cream and use a good exfoliant once or twice a week."

- In your *forties and fifties*, my advice is to get a good derma-tologist, a good facialist, a good sunblock, a good cleans-ing routine, a good moisturizer for day and night, soft lighting, and someone who loves you and makes your laugh lines worth it. There are zillions of anti-aging products to either make you look younger or feel more anxious. I saw an ad for La Prairie Anti-Aging Complex ("a cellular in-tervention cream") and realized I don't *need* an anti-aging complex. I *have* an anti-aging complex.

Health and Beauty, at Any Age
Dr. Marsha Gordon, vice chairman of the Department of Dermatol-ogy, Mt. Sinai Medical Center, and a consultant to *The Today Show,* weighs in: "First, at any age you need protection from the sun. We never want to do damage that will come back to haunt us later. There is evidence that very small amounts of sun cause cumulative damage. We need to be protected from both the burning rays—UVB—and the browning/tanning rays—UVA. UVB protection is easy. This is largely measured by the SPF number, so if we choose a nice high SPF and reapply frequently, we're fine. UVA is more chal-lenging. There is no approved number to measure this. The best sunscreen ingredients for UVA are (1) micronized or superfine zinc, (2) titanium dioxide, or (3) avobenzone (also called Parsol 1789)." Sun protection must include physical protection too—wide-brimmed hats, don't sit in the sun in the midday, et cetera. (Note:

thanks to Dr. Gordon being my doctor, I now get about as much sun as a cremini mushroom. And being blond and fair, I am only allowed to venture out in the sun before 10:00 a.m. or after 4:00 p.m. And don't even *tell* Dr. Gordon that I am going to the Yucatán for six days next January.)

While sun exposure can be damaging, so can any skin inflammation. "This," says Dr. Gordon, "is a more controversial area. But I recommend gentle skin care at all ages. If something in your daily routine is irritating your skin, consider revising the regimen." And finally, from a woman who is as down to earth as she is professionally sophisticated, "Of course, there are all the good things our mothers taught us to keep us healthy that help our skin healthy, too—plenty of fruits and vegetables, enough sleep, and enough physical activity."

Resources

Well, maybe it's just me, but if you ever needed a reason to be glad that you didn't undergo some procedure or if you are a fan of TV's *Nip/Tuck* you'll love www.awfulplasticsurgery.com. There but for the grace of God . . .

It really matters that you do everything under the sun to protect yourself from sun damage. Solumbra (www.sunprecautions.com) offers sun-protective clothes that really make a difference.

EIGHT

Working Out and Shaping Up:
The Zen of the Right Jogging Bra

"Breathe: this lets you live in the moment. Stretch: this releases toxins from your muscles . . . Be creative. Do one thing a day that scares you."

—Lululemon athletica, a highly evolved company with great clothes and a great philosophy

"My life sucks and I'll never look good in Victoria's Secret underwear."

—Fifteen-year-old teenager to her best friend

"If you only have one addiction, it might as well be Pilates."

—Pilates instructor Nancy Jean McNamara

From day one, it is drilled into all of us that anything larger than a size 0 at the Gap is unacceptable, that there are "good" foods and "bad" foods, and that the waiter should take away the bread basket and butter *immediately*. So anything *any woman* writes about bodies and fitness needs to be enlightening, reassuring, motivating, and 100 percent fat-free and guilt-free.

But, hey—we're only human. So this chapter is for all of us who know how important it is to do everything we can to lose weight and look better . . . Oops, I mean, to get *healthier* and start *feeling better, more accepting of our bodies and at peace with ourselves*. Frankly, all of these are worthy goals. And (how many times have you heard this?) you can't *look* great without *feeling* great. And you can't *feel* great unless you take good care of yourself. The exception to this is the small global coterie of seventeen-year-old fashion models who swill champagne before a show and stay up all night afterward partying and never take their makeup off and jet from Moscow to Milan nonstop and never exercise and eat bacon cheeseburgers and *always* look breathtakingly fresh and dewy and beautiful. The moral is: we hate these girls and hope that at least one of them gets a tiny patch of cellulite on her flawless thigh or has her favorite lipstick shade discontinued.

The other 99.9 percent of us has to work hard to stay fit, learn how to de-stress ourselves, and come up with ways to feel good about ourselves. My friend Barbara Harrison simply says, "Learn to accept and even like your body." Another approach is Oprah's: don't accept anything you don't want to. Which works best when you can work with your own trainer, nutritionist, cook, hairstylist, fashion stylist, and God knows what else. In fairness to Oprah, her mantra of "progress, not perfection" always makes sense.

I believe in acceptance *and* major overhauls: a couple of years ago I got sick of yo-yo dieting and cheating on Atkins. (I actually *gained* weight and at the same time was *deathly* afraid of being fat *and* going into renal failure. The worst of both worlds.) So I made an appointment with a highly recommended New York doctor and nutrition specialist to finally lose that baby weight I had been holding on to (Phoebe was a sophomore in college by then so it had been a while) and find a plan for exercise and wellness that I could realistically incorporate into my totally harried life. One meeting with Dr. Jana Klauer gave me the motivation, guidance, and reassurance I needed. Dr. Klauer radiates serenity, knows her stuff, and is so drop-dead gorgeous that you will do anything she asks.

Here are a few of Dr. Klauer's suggestions (she's got a book out called *How the Rich Get Thin*) along with basics about health and wellness and exercise, as well as the usual assortment of my own personally humiliating stories. You probably know most of these tips already. Frankly, none of them is particularly sexy. But they work.

- Want to lose weight? Eat less and exercise more.
- Exercise every day—one hour of aerobic exercise every day. Exercise helps you feel better, stay flexible, improve your balance, helps you fight joint pain, stiffness, and bone loss.

- Working out with weights—free weights or machines—is essential for improving bone density.

- You really are in charge of your diet, your exercise, your life: "Do," as they say in self-help circles, "the next right thing."

- Meditate. Every day. De-stress.

- Don't just *stand* on the people mover in the airport and let it move you—*walk* on it. Fast. Same thing on escalators where you can either walk up (your own free StairMaster!) or extend your heels over the edge of the step you are on and stretch your hamstrings by flexing your foot.

- We all start to lose our ability to balance as we age. So brush your teeth standing on one foot. Or with your eyes closed. Just for practice.

- Don't ever say you are "on a diet." Diets fail. Changing your eating habits for life because you *want* to succeeds.

- How you see your own body is the single biggest determinant of how your daughter sees her own.

WHAT WE EAT

- Chicken *without* the skin.

- Never say, "I'd like it *fried*." And the words *deep-fried* should never come out of your lips.

- *Never* eat a Cinnabon. No matter how hungry or depressed you are. They have 670 calories and 34 grams of fat.

- Food courts in malls and airports are not your friends.

- *Never* wear anything with an elasticized waist. First of all, it's not a great look and most of all, not having to zip something up means you can be sneakily lax about what you're eating.

- "Moderation and balance." I don't think there's a doctor or nutritionist who won't give you this as a mantra. And who could argue with it?

- Before you pay a professional to tell you this, a "handful of nuts" is really just ten or so; not the most nuts you can cram into your fist. And the "average" suggested serving of pasta is *half a cup*. A serving of meat is supposed to be the size of a deck of cards.

- Small lifestyle changes can mean big results over time: Walking just thirty minutes five times a week burns about 30,000 calories (about 8 pounds) a year.

- Fruit is a dessert. All by itself. Eat a banana or a ripe pear after dinner once in a while.

- The mantra from *everyone* who has anything to do with nutrition: avoid processed foods, oversweetened food, empty calories, artificially sweetened anything. Forget chemically sweetened diet soft drinks.

- The best chance you have of having your kids eat healthy foods is if you eat them yourself.

EXERCISE

- Join a gym. All women or coed. Something fancy or something basic like Curves. Make sure it's user-friendly or you won't use it.

- Make sure it's close enough to work or your house that it doesn't take forever to get to or you'll never go.

- Don't go to my friend Darrel's former gym, which is so laid back that he has seen women knitting on the Exercycle.

- Don't go to my former yuppie Type-A gym where gorgeous young women with no visible body fat increase the challenge by running *backward* on the treadmill. My idea of a good day at that gym was when I saw someone older or more out of shape than me.

- Don't read *Gourmet* or *Food & Wine* on the treadmill. Read *Self* and *Fitness and Running*. You don't need to be salivating about a molten chocolate cake with a million calories while you're on the treadmill trying to work off 130 calories.

- Do what you like. Don't do something—like say, Brazilian Butt Lift—if it's just going to make you feel like a klutz.

- Work hard but don't be a lunatic. "You *can* do it," said the enthusiastic novice Pilates teacher at an unnamed spa I could have sued. Being ever agreeable and enthusiastic, not to mention wanting to go all-out to please her, I literally *vaulted* over one of the Pilates apparatuses. Thank God, the startled instructor happened to be standing there to catch me or I would have broken my neck. The lesson seems to be *don't,* as I seem to do with everything in life, blindly throw yourself into it.

- The treadmill gives you an accurate read of calories burned. The elliptical can be off by 20 percent to 50 percent.

- Nutritionists and trainers prefer the treadmill or StairMaster for optimum fat burning and weight loss.

- Clean the machine after you're done—wipe it off with a towel or spritz and towel off your Pilates mat. Pilates studios use tea tree oil to spritz, then rub with paper towels.

- Great big rubber balls are great to use in the gym and have at home. So are Dyna-Bands. So are free weights.

- If you start off every morning at home with some stretching and gentle exercises, you will feel better and be mindful of your body all day. Well, at least until you get to work and can eat a chocolate croissant.

TEN REASONS PEOPLE AT YOUR GYM WILL HATE YOU

1. You wear a lot of fragrance when you work out.

2. You put your workout mat right smack in front of the teacher so no one else can see her clearly.

3. You put your workout mat really, really close to someone else's because you don't appreciate the need for personal space.

4. In a crowded class, you swing your arms open so wide that you hit right into the person next to you.

5. You grunt when you are lifting weights; you hum or sing along to your iPod.

6. You wait right behind someone who is circuit training and ask, "Are you almost done?"

7. You tell the teacher you think she is teaching something the wrong way.

8. You chitchat with a friend next to you on the treadmill or elliptical, disturbing everyone around you.

9. You sign up for an intermediate or advanced class when you are a beginner.

10. You talk really loudly on your cell phone in the locker room even though there is a big sign that says, No Talking on the Cell Phone in the Locker Room.

GOOD MUSIC TO LISTEN TO AT THE GYM, THANKS TO ANIKA CHAPIN

- Any song that makes you think you are a sexy model walking a runway. Especially good are songs that actually tell you this, such as Right Said Fred's "I'm Too Sexy" and Jill Sobule's "Supermodel."

- Any song that makes you think you are a star athlete running to the finish line. Songs taken from movies with sports themes are usually good for this like, e.g., "Eye of the Tiger" or "We Are the Champions."

- Any song that makes you think you are an incredible dancer, steaming up the floor somewhere. For this, I personally go for sultry salsa songs and imagine I'm in a club in San Juan, but my roommate admitted that she listens to classical music on the treadmill, because imagining that she is a prima ballerina dancing a pas de deux is what motivates her.

- Any song that makes you think you are a fabulous cabaret, or even karaoke, singer. Treadmills are much more fun when you can imagine that you are Aretha Franklin belting out "Respect," although given that actually belting out "Respect" on the treadmill is a no-no, perhaps the shower is a better place for this category.

BAD MUSIC TO LISTEN TO AT THE GYM

- Gregorian chants.
- Any song that begins with a line like "Hello, darkness, my old friend."
- When it comes to music, I would add that it is simply impossible to run or power walk to Björk. It just throws you off completely.

Gender-Specific Advice That Probably Won't Surprise You
Dr. Klauer notes that "When a woman follows a doctor-prescribed nutrition program and doesn't lose weight, she blames herself. When a man goes on a diet and doesn't lose weight, he blames his diet doctor."

AGE

After forty, exercise is not optional. Walk, run, work out on machines in the gym, go to group classes, get a personal trainer—do everything and anything you love with some regularity. And the older you are, the more you need to concentrate on flexibility and balance. Buy a big red exercise ball (www.balldynamics.com) and balance on that. Start exercising when you are young and you will never have to try to do a complete overhaul when you are older. I would add, don't be embarrassed by being the oldest, having the most cellulite, or swimming the breaststroke when everyone else is doing an Olympic-speed crawl.

SPAS

Yes.

Seriously, there are so many different types—rigorous, luxurious, boot camp, pampering, meditative. Do your research; word of mouth is good to find one that's right for you—so is a site like www.spafinder.com. Most spas are inclusive, so there isn't a lot of tipping once you get there except for optional beauty treatments and trips. If you're the least bit shy, it can be a lot more fun to go with a bunch of friends or family members.

NINE

Home Sweet...(Finding It, Buying It,
Furnishing It, Planting It, Renovating It,
Selling It, Leaving It)...Home

"Nothing clashes in Miami."

—Barneys creative director Simon Doonan

"Buy the best and you only cry once."

—Ancient Chinese proverb

Phyllis Edelstein's family home repair mantra: "If it doesn't fit, force it."

Where we live means everything. Even a one-year sublet on a tiny apartment is a big deal. Real estate is not like buying a dress. It's a lot harder to return that center hall colonial. And, hey, what's at stake, anyway? Just spending more money than you've probably ever spent before finding a place you can call your own. Then spending time, energy, and *more* money to really *make* it your own—turning it into a nest, a retreat, a home where you feel comfortable and happy and safe. Where there is space and light and quiet and good karma for great dinner parties. A good fit for you and your family/dog/roommate/significant other/little happy baby. An environment that satisfies your needs, reflects your taste, makes you happy to come home to, makes you glad to wake up in, and if you are some combination of smart and lucky, will someday turn into a good investment, too. That's all your home has to do.

While morning glories will no doubt twine their way around

the trellis, the sun will shine in your bedroom skylight every sparkling morning, and the cat will cozy up in the armchair by the fireplace in the afternoon, maybe you shouldn't get too comfy just yet. House and home are the area of your life with more *"if onlys"* and *"what was I thinking?"* than just about any other, with the possible exception of waking up the morning after you slept with your best friend's fiancé after way too many gin and tonics at a weekend house party gone amok.

Infinite regrets ("I *knew* pickling the floor would ruin it"), recriminations ("Didn't you *measure* to see if the armoire would fit up the stairs?"), deeply held fears (wallpaper; grouping pictures; toile), dashed hopes ("If we had just bought that ivy-covered cottage I loved, everything would have fallen into place"), tectonic shocks ("Installing a new sink in the powder room is going to cost what?!") are pretty much inevitable. After all, there's no other area in life where the word *remorse* seems to creep into everything from decoration to renovation.

So this chapter will be as much twelve-step recovery program as a guide to recovering your chairs. You may not even *know* you need it now, but I will help fortify you for the one that got away ("I *told* you we should have gone with the asking price . . ."), help you gain the knowledge and confidence you need to avoid buyer's remorse ("Didn't it seem bigger when it was empty?"), give you the courage to fight bidding wars, the moxie to stand up to real estate agents with an attitude, the diplomatic skills needed to make amends with the contractor you now regret having fired midway through the job, the power to get a plumber to return your call on a holiday weekend, the equanimity to live with the fact that the six small maple trees you just planted *will* totally block your view of the neighbor's dog run but you just might have to wait fifteen or twenty years for this to be a viable solution.

Just so you know, every neurosis in my life (and they're like snowflakes—no two are alike) has come out like a seasonal allergy every time I move or hammer in a picture hook or look at the real estate section of the newspaper. You say "home" and I say "fret." I can worry for hours just about the new living room curtains: *Are they hanging too close to the floor? Not close enough? Are they too sheer? Should I have had them lined? Do they look cheap? Why were they so cheap? Does the brown really go with the pinstripe on the sofa? Clash? Go so well that it's too "matchy-matchy"? Uh-oh, don't they look just like the cheesy ones in the new catalogue? That everybody will have? For half the price? That are some kind of polyester?* And don't even ask me about *curtain rods*—that's a category unto itself. But over the years I have gotten help and gotten better—thanks to friends who performed timely interventions, thanks to designers and store pros I know and trust, thanks to the odd compliment, and thanks to hiring the occasional color expert and interior designer to help and reassure me. Best of all, when *they* advise me, it's *their* fault, not mine if I hate something. I may wind up feeling distress or disappointment, but at least I don't feel guilty.

Lucky for you, I've come up with some basic principles that will let you stress less. Speaking of stress, did I mention that we actually had a feng shui master come to our house to analyze both the house and garden? It was for an article I was doing about the value of feng shui–ing your house and property, but I took it very seriously. Of course, it turned out, according to the traditional *Bagwa* blueprint of feng shui, that our Wealth and Power corner were in the upstairs bathroom, which meant we were literally flushing our money away. I'm not sure we needed a feng shui expert to tell us this since we got a second opinion every year from our accountant that was remarkably similar, but it's always good to get a consensus.

HOUSE RULES. LOOKING. BUYING.

- You can't drive yourself crazy worrying because it's so much more expensive than your last place and what if you lose your job tomorrow and have to sell pencils on the corner? Or because it's not what your mother-in-law would have picked. Or because you are convinced that the little holes in the pantry door are from termites, even though there was a termite inspection before you signed the contract.

- Someone you know will always have a bigger house; a penthouse apartment . . . with a terrace; five glorious acres; a heated pool. And to make it worse, they might not even have *earned* it—they may have "family money" or invested in a hot stock or gotten a big Wall Street bonus. Coveting or competitiveness will eat away at you just like the termites. Munch, munch.

- You won't buy a house without a screened porch. Fine. Wait for the one that has a screened porch. You want a red front door? Paint it red. You're the boss of you.

- Learn the lingo. In a real estate ad, "Needs TLC" or "Handyman's Special" means a wreck. "Cozy" means tiny. "Wildlife abounds" means you are in the middle of nowhere, except for all the deer who are eating their way through your garden and the coyote who is in your field. "Easy access to highway" means you are practically on it and that you can hear the traffic twenty-four hours a day. "Walk to station" means the house is right by the train tracks.

- Get enough helpful opinions to feel informed and confident about your decisions, but do not do a Gallup poll of what your sister, your work colleagues, your college roommate, your mother think. Talk to real estate lawyers, find out about the neighborhood or building, know what's selling or renting in your price range, take as long as you need to look.

- And skip the kind of advice that seems too New York, too California, too New Age, *too too*. There's a lot to be said for Home Depot and a thorough rereading of back issues of *Metropolitan Home, House & Garden,* and *Wallpaper.* And unless you're buying in Hong Kong, you don't really need to feng shui your house. Just say no to your own personal apartment therapist. Meanwhile, check out Maxwell Gillingham-Ryan's terrifically helpful and hip website instead: www.apartmenttherapy.com.

- Houses and apartments have an aura. If you walk in, it feels good and it makes *you* feel good, that is good. Think men; puppies; jeans; the first time you walk on a college campus—is it a good instinctive fit?

- Hope the owner is home when you're looking. I remember seeing a house where the home owner told me (a lover of pools) that we were standing on the exact spot where he and his wife had covered the large terra cotta swimming pool because it was just too much work to maintain and the drainage on the hill was dreadful. We didn't buy the house.

- In even a relatively hot market, it is a myth that owners of a much-coveted house will be persuaded to sell it to the thoughtful would-be buyer who writes a genuine and heart-felt letter laying out his/her intention of lavishing the house with the same love and care the current owners did. The top and bottom line is price.

- Don't buy big just because you can. McMansions are so aesthetically awful, ecologically offensive, and ostentatious. Do you really need eight bedrooms?

HOUSE RULES: IT'S YOURS

- Don't expect to know everything. Or anything. The fact that you weren't born knowing the difference between "cream" and "ecru," a perennial and an annual, doesn't mean you can't lead a rich, full domestic life.

- Spend the money the way you want to. If you want a big kitchen, go for it. Want to hire a landscape architect and put your money into the ground, fine.

- "It's just stuff," to quote my friend and design consultant Heidi Johnston, owner of Yellow Monkey Antiques in Cross River, New York. Heidi sells, lives with, and loves exquisite English and American antiques. But she also understands what's really important in life. And it isn't the soapstone tureen you dropped and broke, the nonpedigreed Oriental runner that you can't yet afford to upgrade, or the apothecary chest you were outbid on at the auction.

- Don't freak out because there are a million color chips in your paint store and twenty sofa and love seat styles at Crate & Barrel. Choosing colors and furniture can be simplified if you think of both as "regional." With this rule of thumb, it follows that Santa Fe style (the weathered ochre washboard) only really works in Santa Fe. And because the light in Santa Fe reads differently than the light in Manhattan, Santa Fe colors *should* be different than Park Avenue ones. A great example of this is looking at Martha Stewart's houses: her Maine house has a New England seacoast vernacular; her shingled Easthampton house is decorated and landscaped in a Long Island great house style; her colonial Bedford, New York, spread reflects the fact that it is the property of landed gentry; her stately Westport house was burnished antiques and Oriental rugs. Her colors seamlessly evoke the history of the house and the region.

- Stop looking at houses for sale after you've just bought your own. If the houses for sale are worse than yours, it's a waste of time. If they're better, it's real estate masochism.

- Home issues can be big and complicated, but financial and creative solutions can be surprisingly simple. You don't need to hire an interior designer or landscape architect or lighting pro—you can usually find one who will just come in for a consultation. There are clearinghouses that help match you up with the right designer if you do decide to hire one. You can often find a pro who comes in just to rearrange what you already have and make some suggestions about sprucing your home up. You can get paint chips, two-ounce samples or colors you just stick on the wall so you can practice getting the shade you want without committing.

- Taking the time to put together a notebook filled with pictures from magazines of rooms and colors and layouts you love will result in a clear picture for you or a pro to decode your taste. And you'll find that, without even knowing who did it, you will choose the same architects, same styles, same designers almost instinctively.

- Doing your homework, not freaking when something doesn't turn out the way you expected, and feeling empowered enough not to let your electrician get away with, "I'll talk to your husband about it" are the emotional goals. Once you've got this all down, you will be able to avoid what I call the Five Stages of Decorating Death: Confusion, Fright, Mild Panic Attack, Extreme Anxiety, and Total Paralysis.

HOUSE RULES: RENOVATING

- I would say it's like childbirth, but ever since the advent of the pain-blocking epidural, renovating is definitely the harder and more painful. Also it lasts a lot longer. The general rule of thumb is that it costs 50 percent more than budgeted and takes twice as long.

- I used to say that few marriages can survive a major home renovation, but then since my marriage didn't even survive a sofa, I stopped saying it. (But I still secretly believe it.) Move out if you can. Or get it done before you move in.

- From my friend Barbara: "One of the biggest problems is the 'whileyas.' That's 'while ya repainting the room, you might as well replace the carpet, change the closet door handles, put in a skylight . . .' "

- On the sunny side, there are words and phrases that you will only need to know once in your life and then you can forget them. My friend's decorator, planning a renovated den, announced, "I see lambrequins here." Huh? "Lambrequins," which sounds like something in an English petting zoo, turn out to be the term for the frame that hides the top of the curtain.

- Also on the other sunny side: When a renovation is finally over, it's not just the *new* space that looks great. The whole house does, because all the furniture and cartons and papers and books that had to be *stored* all over the house are now back where they should be. The house looks clean and orderly and with less stuff all over, it tends to look enormous, too.

- My friend Phyllis went through a yearlong renovation that was supposed to last six weeks and lived to tell about it. Would she do it again? "Oh, yes!" she says. "But," she adds, "it's good that you don't know what you're in for because if you did, you'd never get out of bed in the morning." (There's a microcosm of life.) As for why it took so long and what made it so painful, Phyllis points out the Law of Unexpected Consequences: "Move one thing and dozens of others will be affected. When I built out the study, it meant that the contractor had to move all the pool stuff and the landscaper had to reorganize every tree and shrub." As to what would she do differently? "I'd be much smarter about money. Anyone who says, 'It's only going to cost . . . ' is whistling down the wind. I would have had a second layer of money for the unexpected and the 'May as well do this, too.' " The end of the story? "I have such attachment to a place I already loved. I get so much pleasure just opening the front door. I made it mine and I love it more."

- Never hire a decorator who says, "Oh, I can install a soffit!"

HOUSE RULES: SELLING

- Curb appeal. It's essential. Take away the tabletop clutter. Clean out the closets so they look bigger. Freshen up the paint. Plant geraniums. Broker tip: Skip the bowl of potpourri (since some people are allergic) and boil cinnamon sticks or orange peels so the place smells good.

- Dog odor, cat odor, and smoke are the biggest turnoffs. Many brokers use a product called Odors Away that you can get at the hardware store.

- Don't be home when someone is looking at *your* house. You'll either be hurt when you overhear someone's negative comments or you'll feel insulted.

- A real estate superstition that used to be kind of word-of-mouth and then finally got into the *New York Times* is that if you plant a St. Joseph statue upside down in your yard, you will be guaranteed good luck for your sale. Since our house hadn't sold in three months, I begged Marsha, my friend and broker, to come to our house in January and dig a space in the freezing, snow-covered ground and plant the statue. Which she did. While the house didn't sell until three months later (Marsha says there is no *time* guarantee from this ritual) we did get a high offer, then a higher offer, then a bidding war that resulted in the house selling over the asking price. There are Catholic supply stores in Westchester, New York, that make most of their money from selling St. Joseph statues to brokers. "But," asked my friend Doreen Fox, who was selling her apartment, "what do you do about planting a St. Joseph statue when you don't have a yard?" "Bury it in the soil of a big plant," Marsha advised.

- In a sale by owner, the price is often *higher* than it would be if the house had a broker. This is a well-known "seller's folly." Very often, a real estate agent would have suggested a lower asking price but the owner (loving the house and not knowing the market as well) believes he/she should get more than the market will actually bear. If you sell your own house, you obviously need to understand all the paperwork and legalities involved. With a broker selling your house, you have the security of knowing that someone will pre-screen potential buyers.

DESPERATION, OBSESSION, AND NEEDINESS. AND THAT'S A *BAD* THING?

Being so obsessed with say, getting a particular house before it goes on the market or bidding too much for what seems like the *only* pine blanket chest for your dining room happens to many otherwise sane women. Some will actually sacrifice *everything*—including their family—just for something they desire. Who would go *this* far and sink *that* low?

Well, for me, it started *way* before I had that wonderful "It's just stuff" mantra. And it *was* in New York City where real estate was and is all anybody talks about or covets. In my old apartment building on the Upper West Side, if you heard that an elderly resident had died, you would say to the elevator man, "Oh, I'm so sorry." And then in the next breath, you would murmur, "How big?" Code, of course, for was it an apartment bigger than your own with a river view that maybe you could get. Which is how I began stalking our landlord, Mr. Sagarin. I had met him a few times and coincidentally he was a big opera lover. My then husband worked for the opera. So we just happened to have two amazing seats to a sold-out *La Bohème* with Luciano Pavarotti, which we gave him. Then he took us to lunch to thank us. Then we volunteered to decorate the tree for the building Christmas party. And as time went on, I sent him home-baked cookies and get well cards, and even a Christmas card that depicted Phoebe (who was a nine-month-old baby) propped up on a tiny sled with the cat sitting next to her in front of the building. Both the cat and Phoebe were wearing tiny Santa hats.

Oh, and I occasionally mentioned to Mr. Sagarin that we would love a larger apartment in the building just in case one came along. My major hit came with a song I wrote for him one Christmas. It was recorded by one of my then-husband's colleagues at the opera and is to the tune of "La Donna é Mobile."

We love our little place,
But we've run out of space.
Our hearts are gloomy . . .
Our rooms aren't roomy.
All that it lacks is space.
We've looked and cannot find,
The dream we have in mind.
Molto desperation! *Piccolo* location!
It's just too small!
Too small . . . Too small . . . *Troppo* too small!

(It goes on and builds to a heartrending finale.)

Two months later, we got the call. "Ms. Pierson," said a familiar voice. "A three-bedroom on the river just came up. Would you be interested?" Hmmm . . . let me think about that for one tenth of a nanosecond while I open the champagne bottle with my teeth and look up the number of the moving men.

BEWARE . . .

- The Pottery Barn syndrome: It is so disconcerting when you walk into a friend's house or apartment and really feel you have walked into a photo shoot for the catalogue of Pottery Barn, Crate & Barrel, Domain, Restoration Hardware, Ballard, West Elm. Of course, everything is well designed, but add something of your own sensibility or it's too creepy.

- You could add something from your travels. But then beware catalogues that feature what look like one-of-a-kind treasures gathered from all over the globe (these catalogues always include a humanitarian cause to contribute to, which is commendable). The problem is that I would much rather *find* tiny temple bells or distressed cobalt bowls someplace (Java, Sumatra, Finland) where they actually *seem* one-of-a-kind, not in a catalogue that goes to thousands of people. Things lose their sense of place and soul when you can just get them through an 800 number.

- Separation Anxiety. My friend Barbara has an issue with people who can't bear to part with anything. And she is *tough*. Barbara says, "Don't save things because they might come in handy someday. You won't be able to find it or it won't be in good condition or it won't be what you remember. And meanwhile it will clutter your life and weigh you down with stuff." I am a dedicated thrower-outer and have *never* gotten rid of anything I later regretted shedding.

- Watch out for things that grow. I mean that literally and figuratively. When we moved into a small weekend house, with its wooded and naturally sloping acreage, my then-husband said, "I think I'd like a little garden." "Okay," I said. And this is what he really meant and what we wound up having: a little rock garden, a little kitchen garden, a little rose garden, a little herb garden, a little cutting garden. Plus a walk-in toolshed, underground watering system, and solar greenhouse.

OVERCONFIDENCE/BAD LUCK/THE STRAW THAT BROKE THE CAMELBACK

Sometimes the best way to learn what not to do is from the utterly humiliating *if only* and *what if* personal stories (read: tragedies) of others. That means from me. *If only* we hadn't sold our country house on the *worst* day of the worst month of the year—a day when *The Wall Street Journal* later said housing prices hit *rock bottom* for the entire year. *What was I thinking* when I painted the library *aubergine?*

If only I hadn't gone to the silent auction and hadn't "*won*" the large gray mohair John Saladino sofa that we *didn't need,* that we *couldn't really afford,* that *didn't fit* in the doorway of our 1844 farmhouse, that then had to be *sawed* apart and *put back together* by a "highly recommended company" that then left *a large rip* in the upholstery. The sofa that our two cats *soon discovered* had the best fabric *ever* for a scratching post, that then turned into such a *ripped wreck* we had to *completely* reupholster it only two months later. The moral? You can take the life out of the sofa, but you can't take the sofa out of the living room.

This is the kind of story that you could laughingly say might lead to divorce. Well, the *good* news is that we didn't have to worry about *that* possibility because the *bad* news was that we had already decided to divorce.

DECORATING CLIFFNOTES

- Any piece of new furniture depreciates 50 percent the moment you buy it. And don't count on an antique appreciating to any huge degree unless it is a very special piece. The price you see in the antique store is usually nowhere near what a store or dealer will give you for selling it—and auctions (unless there is some amazing bidding war) are likely to disappoint. So buy it because you love it, not because of resale.

- Never decorate your house like any interior you've seen in a sitcom.

- Sisal carpet always works.

- If you want to hide something—anything from a radiator cover to a bumpy ceiling—paint it flat black.

- Art should stand on its own. It should never be part of the color scheme. Don't buy the seascape because it matches the rug.

- Only *Trading Spaces* can do it for under $1,000, and do you really want a "Matisse" mural in your finished basement?

- Find someone who really *listens:* don't hire anyone who doesn't want to work with you or who is so opinionated you don't get a word in edgewise. I had a French decorator who was incredibly dismissive of my ideas: when I suggested that the armoire she was designing be so simple as to have almost no ornamentation, she looked at me, sniffed, and said in her French-accented English, "That will look like ze dime store!" She was already half done, so I decided to let her finish but made her do it my way. Then when the armoire was built, I coincidentally found a picture of almost *exactly* the same design in a fashion spread in one of the top shelter magazines, which I tore out and sent to her. Take *zat!*

- When you're looking at vintage or antiques, especially in a flea market or at an antique show *anywhere in the world,* ask the dealer, "Is that your best price?" or "Can you do any better?"

REAL ESTATE

- Location, location, location
- Buy the worst house in the best neighborhood.
- From Jack Taylor, marketing executive: "Nobody ever buys anything to keep it the same."
- The rule of thumb is to stretch on your first house. You'll grow into it financially.
- With a house (like clothes shopping), when you say "I'm going to think about it," 90 percent of the time you won't wind up buying it.
- Do look at lots of places; make sure the school next door isn't noisy; find out if they can build a development in the field behind you; come back and see what the street is like at rush hour. Don't take a broker's word for everything; don't compromise on what's important to you.

ORIENTAL RUGS

- Condition, condition, condition
- Whether to buy a new Oriental rug or old? Pros say, "Better a has-been than a never-was."
- Auctions are great places to buy old Orientals, and now that you can bid online it's a lot easier.

THE GARDEN

- It's all about hope.
- The most common mistake with houseplants is overwatering.
- Every perennial is a weed somewhere.

- "The first year it sleeps, the second year it creeps, the third year it leaps."
- You can prolong the life of cut flowers by removing all the foliage below the water line when you put them in the vase.
- An annual is a plant that grows one season and dies (e.g., petunias and pansies). A perennial comes back every year; they can last for years or for generations. Roses, irises, and peonies are perennials.
- Be careful with wisteria, bamboo, and ivy! All are invasive. Some bamboo will eat your house. Wisteria just nibbles.

MOVING MEN AND INSTALLATION PEOPLE

- Research moving companies. Get references. Make sure you will have an experienced crew who has worked together before.
- Just because someone tells you they can do something and they seem professional, be a little cautious. We once had two guys who were musicians installing a washer/dryer unit and soffit in our laundry room. What should have taken a few weeks took a few months. When they finally got it done, I overheard one telling the other, "I *told* you we should have read the manual."
- If someone at a party says, "And I couldn't have done it without the electrician who figured out the most insane wiring," march right over and beg for the guy's number. If you have friends who are architects or antique shop owners or handymen who love to fix up their own houses, you're in luck because these are the people most likely to know the best resources. Bartering resources is what makes the world go 'round.

FURNITURE FOR NOVICES

- Starter furniture is the kind that doesn't own *you*. Of course, it has to be practical, functional, comfortable, and stylish. What it *doesn't* have to be is something pricey you will want to keep forever. Ikea, Target, and West Elm are good sources.

- When you have outgrown the apartment with five room-mates and are on your own, the pieces that make sense to invest in are dining room and bedroom furniture.

- You can't usually negotiate in a department store, but you can in an independent store.

- To save money, go into a store with a friend or relative. You're more likely to get a discount on the mattress if your sister is buying the same one at the same time.

- Department stores are usually more expensive than inde-pendent or online sources because of the markups. And they won't always have what you want because they have less space for furniture.

COLORS

- There are no bad colors.
- Most color rules are dumb.
- The most fun you can have these days is getting a made-to-order color mixed at your local paint store and then picking the name. My friend Marsha has Florence Mar-sha Gray. And she is the only person in the world who does.

- Murphy's Law: If you leave the brown paint for the shutters and the gray paint for the deck with the painters, tell them which is which before you go to work and make *extra* sure it's clear by leaving a note then calling from the office to see how everything is going, then when you get home the gray paint will be on the shutters and the brown paint will be on the deck.

- For apartments in New York, there is actually a color called Landlord Yellow (don't use it—it's lead based).

Bad Taste Is a Crime: From the *New York Times*

South Africa: Modern, Accented in Bold Bloodshed

A thirty-seven-year-old man told a court how he hacked to death his interior designer because she criticized his décor, local newspapers reported. The man, Jose de Silva, pleaded guilty to killing forty-seven-year-old Beatrice Harrowyn in 2001 after inviting her to his new home in an upscale suburb of Johannesburg. "We went through the house and I told her what I wanted," he said. "She did not make any nice comments about my place, so I went to my garage and fetched an ax." He is expected to be sentenced on Tuesday.

RESOURCES

www.benjaminmoore.com

www.moss.com

www.designsponge.blogspot.com

www.finnishdesignshop.com

Metropolitan Home—Decorate: Insider's Tips from Top Designers, Michael Lassell (Filipacchi Publishing)

Metropolitan Home—Renovate: What the Pros Know About Giving New Life to Your House, Loft, Condo or Apartment, Fred Bernstein (Filipacchi Publishing)

www.consumerreports.org

TEN

I Gave at the Office: Working, Careers,
Volunteer Work, Offices, Bosses, Success,
Never Flying Middle Seat in Coach
on a Business Trip

"Every woman is a working woman."

—Chinese saying

"Nothing makes you look like a million bucks like a million bucks."

—www.womenandco.com, a women's financial advisory group

"If you really do put a small value on yourself, rest assured the world will not raise your price."

—From a church bulletin board in New York City

"All I want is a warm bed, a kind word, and unlimited power."

—Slogan on a T-shirt worn by a friend's twenty-two-year-old daughter

"Opportunity is not a lengthy visitor."

—Stephen Sondheim

For me, the right career path is the one where you can best use all your skills and talents, fly business class to meetings in Paris, and make someone hate you at your tenth high school reunion. The whole point of work is to make it work for *you*. Which means finding the right career, the right fit, then knowing how to get everything you want out of it.

My credentials and my career story: I do not believe that you need to be young and fresh to have young, fresh ideas and think in contemporary terms. On the other hand (and perhaps because I am secure enough and successful enough not to care), I like to think of myself as the oldest living woman in advertising. When people in my office (most of whom were born after 1980) ask when I started in the business, I usually reply, "When dinosaurs roamed the earth." The point isn't that maybe someday I will get a gold watch. The point is that I am a survivor and have managed to stay afloat against all odds in a field where the median age is twenty-three. I have always worked in large global companies where performance was everything and you were only as good as your last whatever. And on top of that, I have a side career in publishing and in between all that, managed to do things like commute, raise children, and make chicken pot pies from scratch (with little cut-out pastry chickens marching around the top) for dinner parties. You might ask, "How?" Or, as many of my friends do, you might ask "Why?"

1. I love to work.

2. I have gotten a lot in return: from a good salary to an understanding of what makes people tick to learning how to negotiate to developing a work ethic that underlies everything in my life to going everywhere from Belize to Berlin to learning to use *expense* as a verb, as in, "Let's get the lobster salad. I can expense it."

3. My daughter Phoebe (a hard worker) *never* wants to work in the corporate world. Of course, I did tell her, starting from her first conscious moments, "Never go into advertising" and repeated this for the next sixteen years.

One of my heroes in the business world is Ben Stein, the multitalented economist, lawyer, writer, and actor who seems to grasp and articulate the workings of this world with a rare combination of experience, common sense, and perspective. In his recent *New York Times* column, entitled "O.K. Freshmen, It's Time to Study the Real World," Mr. Stein talks to students about what is really going to matter to them, starting right now. "In college," he advises them, "you are given the privilege of learning two incredibly important tasks: to work and to think. Clear thought will guide you all your life, especially in your work and investment decisions." He adds: "Even more vital is the ability to work. Many college students think that work is slavery and captivity. Far from it. Labor is dignity, mental health, a grasp on reality. Freud said that nothing grounds a person so powerfully in reality as putting emphasis on work." I can only add that this point on work sometimes takes a while to sink in.

I have a friend whose fifteen-year-old daughter started a summer job at a neighborhood boutique. "How did it go?" her mother asked after the first day. *"Awful,"* her daughter replied. "Gary made me refold all the jeans and clean up the stockroom. He was *so* bossy. Who does he think he is?" "Your *boss*," said her mother.

Work is good. What kind of work is good for you? There are women like me who love working for big companies: we get steady paychecks, health benefits, the ability to move inside a large global network, the excitement and dynamism of a mix of people and accounts. The downside? Not feeling in control—if everyone is working a fourteen-hour day to get a presentation ready, so are we. Not getting to the gym because there's a meeting at noon and everyone has to be there. Having to be a team player even when I don't agree with their politics or agenda.

Then there are women who work for big companies but who rarely go into the office. I have a friend who works for IBM but who only goes into her office once a month. The rest of the time she works at home on her computer. The upside? She doesn't have to commute, go into the office, have people breathing down her neck. But the hard part for her, as it is for anyone who works at home even part-time, is feeling isolated, missing being part of a team, having to figure out the boundaries between her personal life and her work life, needing the discipline to start at 9:00 a.m. and work straight through without checking her email fifty times.

There are the artists and writers and full-time mothers and entrepreneurs and dog walkers and massage therapists who share the same lack of structure and who have to create it for themselves. With all the freedom comes personal responsibility and the wonderful/scary realization that no one is going to tell you what to do.

There are women who work for small companies who have the advantage of never feeling overwhelmed, of knowing everyone and everything, of being part of a well-connected network. The downside is that working with so few people can be constricting and feel more like a gossipy, cliquey suburban neighborhood than a global village.

There are also the glamour professions, where you can be a glamorous personal assistant to a glamorous record company executive and make almost nothing. Or get a trainee job at a prestigious auction house and realize that you need a trust fund to afford to live on the pittance of a salary. Or you could be an actor—balancing auditions, acting classes, and trays of martinis for the part-time cocktail waitress job that helps you make ends meet. There's an old joke: First guy: "I'm an actor." Second guy: "What restaurant?"

Mr. Stein says something it took me years to realize. "High earnings are largely a function of choosing the right field. Or, as Warren Buffett said in an annual report years ago, 'It is far better to be ordinary in a great business than to be great in a mediocre business.' " Mr. Stein adds, "Over the years I have seen it. Smart men and women in finance and corporate law always grow rich, or at least well-to-do. Incredibly smart men and women in short-story writing or anthropology or acting rarely do."

- *Health* magazine recently noted that about a third of all employees forfeit vacation time. The truth is that the company will not fall apart without you; that vacations are good for your health, make you more productive, and bring a new perspective to your job. The wonderfully paradoxical nature of a high-pressure job is that the more stressed your job makes you, the more justified you can feel for going off to a spa in Mexico and getting hour-long hot stone massages.

- If you work in a stressed, high-pressure corporate job, go to the gym in the morning *before* work. You will feel saner and also be less likely to be angry with the powers that force you to go from meetings to deadlines to a conference call to 8:00 p.m. and no end in sight.

- If you are working on your own, make sure you are doing for yourself what a company would do for you. Set aside money for vacation; put money into an IRA; give yourself a vacation schedule. A psychotherapist friend who works at home told me that the best advice she ever got from her accountant was: "Your practice is your business."

- If you work at home, get involved and stay in touch with the outside world. Do a lot of networking. Pick up the phone. Put other stuff in your life—get connected to a professional organization, a church, a charity, a coed gym.

- Working on your own also means that your days feel like they never end. You're likely to be working long hours or thinking about projects all day and into the evening. Set your own "office hours" and stick to them.

HOW WORK WORKS EVERYWHERE

Every job is different, but the principles remain the same. And while some of the following may sound too simple, it's just because most businesspeople (speakers, writers, consultants) make it all seem so complicated, use big words and complicated theories and mumbo jumbo about moving your cheese or parachuting. I just went to a conference where they were talking about "micromanaged granulated thinking." All I could relate that to was granulated sugar.

- Work is hard work. But Ben Stein is wise to note that "Those who are happiest are the ones who work regularly and diligently."

- Very few people start any new job or enter a career feeling supremely confident. Most of the ones who do are arrogant jerks. In truth, you build confidence little by little. It comes from feeling that you know what you're supposed to be doing and that you are doing it well. It comes from seeing that other people—even the ones way far more experienced than you—don't always know what they're doing either. It comes from feeling that you are in control.

- Success comes from confidence.

- Confidence and success come from realizing that you have a lot to offer and feeling that you are deserving. Of respect. Of a chance to prove yourself. Of being given the opportunity to try something you've never done before. Of being treated like a professional.

- Success breeds success.

- Make connections. Network. Networking obviously helps you get a foot in the door, a recommendation that carries a lot of weight, and an ally in a tough business world. But it is a two-way street: you will repay a mentor with your professionalism and performance. And someday you will mentor someone else.

- Don't get too rattled or too anxious. Don't give the people who run your department or your company (usually men) the power to decide your worth. *You* know when you're doing a good job. *You* know when it's the assignment that is the problem or when your bosses are idiots. You are *not* as good as your last assignment. Don't let anyone let you believe that.

- Be pragmatic. Liz Grossi Strianese says, "The fact is there is no one perfect job, and it's virtually impossible to have your love life, apartment, and job in sync all at once."

- Psychotherapist Phyllis Cohen suggests a way of dealing with someone in the office who makes you crazy or who isn't a fan of yours. "Use reverse psychology. If they're bullying or intimidating or provocative, know that they are doing it on purpose. So be nice to them and you'll throw them off completely."

- Don't work for someone who is abusive. Life is too short. And no matter how junior you are, you don't have to take it.

- Your own opinion of your performance is more important and more accurate than anyone else's. Set your own standards.

- Everyone has days (weeks) when they hate their job and their boss and can't figure out why they are there.

- Thank your dad. If he is one of those fathers who imprinted on you from day one that you are bright and worthy and full of wonderful things to offer, you are the luckiest girl in the world. Every review of top women CEOs comes to the same conclusion: the most successful women in business have fathers who applauded and supported them every step of the way.

WHAT NOT TO BELIEVE

- Don't believe those CEOs who tell you they only sleep three hours a night. You know, the ones who swear they are up jogging or writing their latest novel by 5:00 a.m. Very few actually are.

- Don't believe the people who tell you that you can't be a mother *and* have a career. Of course, you can. Will you feel sane and balanced and guilt-free? Probably not, but so what? Go for it. Are there jobs that give you more flexibility and make it easier to do both? Sure, but not many.

- Don't believe that what the human resources person *swears* you are about to tell her is confidential *will* be confidential. I've seen far too many HR people be incredibly indiscreet. Not to be paranoid, but don't trust anyone unless you absolutely know you can or unless you have something on them that you can use.

- Don't believe that upper management does their own time sheets, never takes pay raises, eats every day in the company cafeteria, flies coach. They just *want* you to believe that.

- Don't believe that just because the guy in the next cubicle went to Harvard he is smarter than you are. And you are allowed to hate anyone who offhandedly says, "Oh, I went to a small liberal arts college in Boston" and it turns out to be Harvard.

- Don't believe a well-meaning mother who thinks you should cut your nails shorter so you can type better or a father who asks you, "What's the point of success if you don't have anyone to share it with?"

THINGS THEY DON'T TEACH YOU
AT BUSINESS SCHOOL

- From television production executive Marjorie Kalins: "Just because the person in authority is a man doesn't mean that he knows what he is doing."

- People will tell you "Don't go into *that* career or *that* company—it's so *political*." *Every* business or profession or corporation is political, from advertising to museum work to nonprofit to academia to (surprise) politics.

- From planning consultant Marylin Silverman: "Don't ever say 'thank you' for your raise. Say, 'That's terrific.' You don't have to be so thankful for something you deserve."

- Also from Marylin: "When you are discussing raises or bonuses with your boss, state your case; prove by the facts of your performance that you deserve *something;* then end your part of the conversation with, "So what can I expect?" That guarantees your boss can't end with a vague, "Let me think about it" or "I'll get back to you."

- Don't be a victim. Don't always be the one who will FedEx the package at 1:00 a.m., who volunteers to collect the money for the office party, who stays to clean up after a lunch meeting. You will only be rewarded by being the go-to girl for terrible, thankless office jobs.

- It's not how much you make, it's how much you keep.

- Followed by this from Ben Stein: "If you are old enough to have sex, you are old enough to start saving in a sensible way for your retirement . . . invest for it early and in a sensible, highly diversified way." And if you're like me and can barely figure out what those buttons on the calculator do, call a financial consultant or work with someone who is really smart about money.

- The closer you live to the office, the later you'll be for work.

- Dress for the job you want to have, not the job you have now.

- Don't interrupt. When someone is talking in a meeting, let him/her finish. The utter brilliance of what you are about to say will never outweigh your rudeness, lack of respect, and insensitivity.

- Don't ramble. Be succinct. Get to the point. Women tend to ramble more than men.

- When in doubt, reboot. And RTFM (read the f***ing manual).

- There are great business expressions and acronyms. My new favorite is a British one, FILTH, which means "Failed in London? Try Hong Kong."

- Do not believe your client is your friend. You can be friendly with clients and go out to dinner with them. But these are *business* people who go by the bottom line. And they will (not unkindly and not without some remorse) ditch you if they think someone else can handle their business better than you can.

- Successful book editor Diane Reverand: "Don't look for friends in the office. Don't confide in someone you don't know well enough to trust." I would add, don't share your life story in the office. Don't ask personal questions.

- The definition of insanity: "Keep doing the same thing and expect the results to be different" holds especially true at work. If your boss doesn't praise you now, even though your work is fantastic, he/she never will. If your client has never been satisfied with *anything,* don't expect a big "wow!" It's not a case of lowering your expectations as much as knowing things are the way they are.

- Be kind and decent to everyone from the junior member of the team to the mailroom guy. Some of these people will eventually soar to some stratospheric position and remember you affectionately. The mailroom guy will always get your FedEx out in time. Your secretary will do your expenses for a two-week trip to Thailand and tell everyone that you had an appointment when you've really just overslept.

- "Women," observes advertising executive Antonia Green, "can read a room better than men."

- We drilled it into Phoebe from around the time she started nursery school, but it still holds true: "Firm handshake and look them in the eye."

DON'T BE A GIRL.

I would urge you not to volunteer for making coffee, not being the first one in the room for the meeting (somehow only *women* show up right on time), and not asking a question by asking a question. As in, "Could I ask a question?" before you actually do ask one. Do not end your sentences with questions: e.g., "I've done the research and the qualitative results are quite shocking?" If someone asks why you don't feel well, never say "cramps" or "PMS." Do not display family photos, crystal bunnies, tiny carved Mexican angels, swatches of your bridesmaid dress, or nail polish on your desk or in your work space. "Do not," says Doreen Fox, advertising executive and mother of two, "leave your breast pump out on your desk with the door open." Do not keep your cell phone on in the office, especially if it mews like a kitty when it rings. Do not have a screensaver or mousepad of you and your family at Christmas. Don't come in from lunch with big shopping bags from sample sales. Don't let the guys in your office get away with telling dirty jokes or being obnoxious because you want to be liked—you're not running for Miss Congeniality. Do not cry in the office unless you absolutely have to and then cry only behind a closed door. Do not be a little gossip or a snitch. Don't be a little suck-up. Don't show an embarrassing amount of cleavage. Do not set the workplace back twenty years for the rest of us.

RESOURCES

Any book by Deborah Tannen, professor of linguistics at Georgetown University, who writes about decoding what people are saying, what they really mean, human dynamics, the difference between how women speak and how men speak. It's not just reading in between the lines; it's learning to listen to people in a social or office situation and really understand where they are coming from.

Read smart women who write smart columns: Anna Quindlen in *Newsweek* and Maureen Dowd in the OpEd page of the *New York Times* are both clear and lucid and neither hesitates to say what she really thinks.

Women who have real, sometimes messy, fully dimensionalized lives are the ones to learn from: Doris Lessing; Anne Lamott; Renée Fleming on her career and life; Azar Nafisi, author of *Reading Lolita in Tehran*. These are all women who all figured out a lot that can be applied to relationships and to careers. These are women who are willing to share their failures and successes.

NON-RESOURCES

There are a ton of "business" books and many business features on television—the author or star is often someone with a huge ego or a good PR agent. Or she is married to a man of some importance and has decided she is important in her own right. Even if she is really bright and has a lot to share, her tone tends to be self-congratulatory and "enough about me, what do *you* think of me?" Think Ivana Trump, Kathy Hilton, Suzy Wetlaufer Welsh, Kathie Lee Gifford. Steer clear.

Ditto those aggressive art of war books by obscure ancient Chinese generals that men seem to think hold huge deep messages for business today.

ELEVEN

Dealing **with** the Pros Like a Pro:
Your Shrink, Your Car Mechanic,
Your Gynecologist, Your Lawyer,
Your Dry Cleaner, Your Exterminator,
Your Vet

Me: "How do you get a plumber to call you back on a Saturday?"
Architect Jerome Kerner: "It's easier to get *the* Pope to call you
back on a Saturday!"

"I'm ruled by my deliveries."

—My friend Phyllis in the middle of traumatic yearlong
residential renovation

If you think a good *man* is hard to find, well, then
you haven't tried to find an air-conditioning repairman or plumber
or psychotherapist lately. These are the gifted people who can make
your house cool, your shower warm, your head sane, your roaches
dead, your buttons stay on. In short, the ones who can add immea-
surably to the quality and pleasure of your life. And do all the
messy jobs you either *can't* or hope you *won't* ever have to.

The corollary is: if you are not nice (*really* nice) to these people
or do not play by their rules, *they can make your life a living hell.*
No question: they are indispensable and their services are invaluable. Which is probably how they figured out that the more they
charged, the more we would value them; that the harder they were
to get in touch with, the more fiercely we would hit redial; that the
longer they kept us waiting, the more grateful we would be to get
an appointment. Shrinks, for example, figured out that if *every sin-*

gle shrink in America took off the entire month of August and went to Wellfleet, Massachusetts, we would all be begging for a 9:00 a.m. appointment the Tuesday after Labor Day.

You are likely to have some of your most intimate relationships with these people (shrinks, gynecologists, and plumbers), see them every day for weeks on end (contractors, real estate agents, house painters), deal with them on an ongoing basis (dog walkers, root canal specialists, house painters, dry cleaners), rely on them for things that can make you or break you (hairdressers, accountants, telephone repairmen, personal trainers, the travel agent who is booking your trip to Shanghai via Sydney on frequent flyer miles, the snowplow guy), rely on them to take good care of what's most precious to you (your pedicurist, your kids' teachers, your exterminator).

A few issues to consider: How do you find the best people in every category? Sometimes, it's just luck or serendipity. A friend says, "I once chose a dentist because the sign outside his office read, 'Dr. Plaque.' This proved to be a more reliable method than the next time I needed a dentist, when I did my research and asked a neighbor for a recommendation and got someone far less satisfying."

My own story. When Phoebe was eight or so, I chose a dentist for her because Dr. Whatever (I've blocked out his name) had a bunch of impressive diplomas in his office, loved cats (we love cats), told me he was a big opera lover (we are big opera lovers), and came as a referral from *my own dentist*. All went swimmingly until the day I came to pick her up from a routine checkup—she had gone there with Enid, her nanny/other mother—and Phoebe announced that Dr. Whatever had *yanked* a tooth out of her mouth. He hadn't told me he was doing an extraction. *"Yanked?"* I asked her. "Yes," she said. "Well, first he pulled and twisted to get it loose enough to come out. Then he yanked it with his hands." "With his *hands*?" "Yup." "But he gave you novocaine, right?" "No," said Phoebe. "Nothing." Well, forget the fact that we all loved *Turandot* and calico cats. *I* didn't share his love of sadistic pain-filled child-abusive dentistry. So all the research and recommendation and relationships in the world don't protect you from making mistakes.

Another issue is that we all want to be self-sufficient and competent but we also need to strike a balance between what we can do for ourselves, what we don't have time for, and what would be sheer folly to attempt. A friend reassuringly suggests, "We don't have to be experts in everything. This is the 'superwoman' idea and it should be put to bed once and for all. Get AAA, hire an accountant, get a computer specialist, find a really good yuppie take-out place, let someone hem your pants. Being a working woman, a mother, a wife, a daughter, or any combination of the above is enough for any woman." Amen.

THE BEST MAN (OR WOMAN) FOR THE JOB

- If you can, use referrals from friends or colleagues to find someone for the job. "Don't," says a friend who is a real estate agent, "take a number off a truck. People," she says, "get desperate about plumbers and electricians."

- Liz Grossi Strianese says what everyone echoes: "You pick the best by word of mouth. I'm always asking people where they got their hair done or who tailored their skirt. Usually, the really good people don't need to advertise because their dockets are full. The irony, of course, is that if they're too busy to see you, they're the ones you want to see."

- How do you get a prime-time appointment? From a retired doctor: "Try to get to know one or two staff people by name—occasionally bring them a little box of chocolates or a bunch of flowers from your garden."

- A *new* customer or patient goes to the back of the line. When we moved to the suburbs we were last on the list of the snowplow guy so we were the very last to get our driveway plowed. Very often, he showed up at 4:00 a.m. when he was so exhausted he tore out piles of gravel from our driveway along with removing the snow. We didn't complain. The next year he came at 2:00 a.m. and tore out a lot less of the driveway.

- Whether it's a house cleaner or a radiologist, ask enough people you trust, who they use or recommend and the same two or three names will keep coming up.

- Use someone who lives in your town or someone who is associated with a brand name. That way, they're a lot more accountable. And findable.

- Get the snowplow guy signed up in the summer. Sign up the pool guy in the winter.

- If you need an appliance fixed, consider logging on to the company's website and see if they have a list of service people in your area.

- Do your homework. Find out how the real estate agent did last year. Was she so successful she was in the Platinum Circle at her company? Does your accountant understand your business? Does the guy who is going to deliver your antique furniture have a dented truck?

- A friend who has a city apartment and a country house advises, "Never have friends do a job for you. Frequently it's unsatisfactory and it's a great way to lose a friend." Ask me how the washer our out-of-work musician friends installed worked.

- From someone who has a huge house that demands a lot of upkeep: "Get top people. Pay them on time. Stay their customer—don't switch around. If they send an employee who is extraordinary, tip him or her. These are the people who will *want* to come back and work for you."

- Architect Jerome Kerner says, "My women clients tend to go into showrooms, look at fixtures or tiles, then talk to vendors about projects and resources like plumbers and tile guys—that's a good starting point." The store looks good for knowing reputable people and the potential customer feels that this is a store she can trust and do business with.

- Look for someone who is passionate about his or her profession. We once had an exterminator named Mr. Mitch who worked for a company called Ex-Pest. What I loved about Mr. Mitch was that the moment he came into the apartment, he snuck into the kitchen and scuttled all over on his back, holding a flashlight to check on any possible activity. "I *think* like a roach," was Mr. Mitch's proud refrain.

DO YOU LIKE THEM? DO THEY LIKE YOU? IS THIS THE RIGHT MATCH? TIPS AND WARNINGS

- Once you find someone you like, do everything to hold on to them. Chat, let them know you are glad they're on the job, inquire about their families, laugh at their jokes, pay cash, offer a glass of water.

- Don't ever get into the position of letting a doctor call you by your first name while you have to call him or her "Doctor So and So."

- Ask the doctor's receptionist to call you if the doctor is running more than fifteen minutes behind schedule. If you can't get the appointment time you want, ask to be called if there is a cancellation.

- If someone—a hairdresser, a doctor, a computer technician—*always* runs late, switch.

- If your potential plastic surgeon doesn't have the latest *Vogue, Harper's Bazaar,* and *W* in the office, go see someone else.

- If you go to the architect's house and hate it—the rooms are too small; it's all full of stuff and nothing quite goes together—there's a clue.

- If you can find someone who makes you well *and* makes you laugh, you have it made. Being half-Jewish and half-Protestant, this story has particular resonance to me. I was in the office of the truly wonderful Dr. Steven Gruenstein, just sitting there, while he was looking at a drug company's website to see if a particular drug had any possible side effects that would make it a bad choice for me. After waiting for a few minutes (and always looking at the big picture), I said to him, "Listen, just tell me if I'll gain weight with this drug." He laughed and said that in his experience, his patients broke down in two categories. All his Jewish patients asked if they would *gain weight* with the drug. And all his non-Jewish patients wanted to know if they could still *drink* if they took the drug. Actually, after my question about weight gain, I was going to ask if I could still drink with this particular drug, but I was too embarrassed.

- Be creative. From a friend who has renovated and remodeled many times over a twenty-five-year marriage: "Set a fake deadline. 'I *have* to leave by three gets the washing machine delivered sooner than if they think you'll be home all day." And she suggests: "Be *dramatic*. 'We have a funeral at noon. I'm expecting one hundred people back at my house and the kitchen faucet handle just broke off in my hand!!!' worked gangbusters for me."

TOOLS YOU'LL USE

Screwdriver: You can fake a hammer, but you cannot substitute anything for a screwdriver. Make sure to get one that has both flat-head and Phillips head noses and comes in at least two different sizes. They make cool ones that have all these things in one.

Hammer: Okay, so you can sort of fake a hammer. A friend of Phoebe's says, "I once saw my roommate install a blackboard using the heel of her J. Crew flats on the nails—but when it comes down to it, you're going to need the real thing. Besides, don't forget the *back* of the hammer—you'll need to pull nails out at some point, and those flats just aren't going to cut it, no matter how pointy the toe." Parenthetically, my friend Marsha sagely notes that while you can kill just about any bug with the heel of say, a loafer, you can't kill a bug using driving shoes since the bottom of driving shoes isn't flat—it's got those little concave spaces between the raised dots.

Pliers: Another one you need, probably for a myriad of things you can never truly predict (earring hook repairs, opening stuck nail polish bottles) as well as those you can (assembling and disassembling furniture and shelves).

Tape measure: If you have furniture, and you have walls, you will need a tape measure. Or, if you're in a good mood, measure your waist.

The number of a plumber/handyman/super/guy: Ultimately, it may save time and expense if you just add the speed dial and skip the *wrench*. Wrenches don't make sense if you don't know what to do with them, and when your toilet starts gushing water, you don't want to learn by trial and error.

HIRING A CONTRACTOR

- Like everything else, word of mouth. Or rely on the advice of your architect.

- From my friend Doreen: "Don't hire the contractor who is missing a finger."

- Find out how busy the contractor is. How many guys does he have working for him (I know it could be a "her")? If it's only two, you'll see why a three-week job can take nine weeks. Will he *tell* you that he has only two guys working for him? "No," says a veteran architect. Many residential contractors don't have an office staff. So you could leave messages until you're blue in the face. Get his cell phone number. If he won't give it to you, don't use him.

WORKING WITH A CONTRACTOR

- Never assume anything. Get it in writing.

- Sometimes, it costs more because the sink was two inches too wide to fit, which delayed the tilework, which held up the backsplash, which . . . Most contractors are good at making delays seem like they're not *their* fault. And if you've been camping out in the living room with your kids for four weeks, eating take-out, the word *delay* is not what you want to hear.

- Sometimes hearing or reading other people's stories can make you feel better about your own. The one not to miss is www.ContractorsFromHell.com—as good as www.bad plasticsurgery.com and just what it sounds like. It was started by a California woman whose contractor broke a pipe that leaked deadly carbon monoxide into her house, installed the tar paper backward so it captured water instead of repelling it (the moisture spawned toxic mold), and caused the house to flood when he left a huge unseen hole in the ceiling. Her site educates home owners about to start their own renovation projects and shares horror stories.

- Keep mentioning to your contractor that you have lots of friends who need work done.

- Alternately, mention that a lot of your friends and relatives are lawyers.

- Never pay in full, up front. And don't even finish payment when the job is done—wait a week or two to make sure everything is really working and is glitch-free.

HOW TO GET THE MOST OUT OF SOMEONE WHO HAS MORE DEGREES THAN YOU DO OR WHO TAKES TWENTY MINUTES JUST TO BLOW-DRY YOUR HAIR

- Be open. Just because your hairstylist has twelve visible piercings and her hair is the color of strawberry Jell-O, doesn't mean she's going to give you a punk look while you want a blunt-cut bob. And just because your shrink dresses like early Judy Collins, wears fringed serapes and hand-carved wooden necklaces from Guatemala, and fills her office with spider plants in macramé holders and tiny happy Buddhas doesn't mean she won't be a wise and wonderful person who understands the siren song of designer sample sales.

But:

- If a shrink calls you by another person's name, he or she just might not be as tuned into you as you would like.

- The four biggest things women don't like to talk to their shrinks about: Sex, especially kinky sex or kinky sex dreams. Any plastic surgery they might have had. Money (if they get a raise or an inheritance, they're afraid the shrink might raise their fee). Anything flattering about people in their lives who they have previously trashed in therapy (it will force them to reexamine and rethink everything they have already spent time hashing out). And according to my friend Alexis Johnson, women clients often don't tell their shrinks when they are going out with a famous married man.

- If you've got medical issues, get second opinions. And a third opinion. But don't get so many opinions that the advice is contradictory and you are confused. And don't just find the person who gives you the opinion you *want* to hear.

- Before you choose a doctor, have a consultation.

- If you're not happy with the service or results—whether it's a car tune-up or a slipcover or a medical procedure—speak up. And if you're not happy with the response you get, speak to a supervisor, write a letter to management, stop your check, *do* something.

- Negotiate a fee or question a bill if it seems like it's too much for the work done; more than you expected; not at all what you were *led* to expect. Get an itemized bill.

- Tip well. If you don't know the going rate, ask. Tip everyone you want or need to at the holidays. Again, if you're not sure, ask around. *Gift* well, too. Whether it's a gift certificate or a pair of freshwater pearl earrings, make sure you thank the people who have taken good care of you all year: your personal trainer, your hairstylist; your office travel agent.

- You know when you need a haircut or when to bring your car to the shop. How do you know when you're ready to terminate psychotherapy? Shrinks usually look for cues from their clients first. And clients usually know by instinct. Alexis Johnson says that a rational question to ask is: "Is my life in pretty good shape and where I want it to be? And if there are things I'm working on changing, are they things I can change on my own or could I use some professional help?"

YOU KNOW IT'S NOT GOING TO WORK IF . . .

- Someone makes you feel bad. My friend Jane went to a new hairstylist who said to her: "This new style will make you look much younger." She hadn't *asked* him for something to make her look younger.

- Phyllis Cohen was getting ready for her renovation. "When I was picking tile for my bathroom," she remembers, "I told the tile installer that I loved the terra cotta colors because they reminded me of Italy. He replied that he had seen some tile just like it in the south of France when he stayed at a really charming Relais & Châteaux Hotel. That's when I knew this wasn't going to be an inexpensive job and he might not be the one for me."

- You know more about your shrink's life than she knows about yours. My ex-shrink told me (while I was paying) snippets about her trip to Africa, her summer home in Maine, and the New Year's Eve she spent in Rome—the whole dinner menu, too.

- Your doctor is an asshole. My friend Grace has a story about how you just know when to switch. Her mother had been getting recurring migraines and the whole family was increasingly concerned. Finally, her mother went to a neurologist who listened to her entire medical history and before *he did a single test,* said to her, "It's probably a tumor."

- Your time can't be valuable to anyone who puts you on

hold for a long time and keeps playing the message that says, "Your time is very valuable to us."

RESOURCES

www.cartalk.com: Two professional mechanics—and funny, funny guys—from Cambridge, Mass., answer all your car questions on NPR in one of the most popular shows on radio.

www.carfax.com: How to find out everything about the used car you are considering. Gives you and the dealer (and most dealers will access it while you are at the dealership) what you need to know about previous repair work and accident records.

Help, It's Broken! A Fix-It Bible for the Repair-Impaired, by Arianne Cohen (Three Rivers Press).

TWELVE

Travel: Getting Away from It All.
Well, Maybe Not Too Far from an
Ionic Hairdryer, a Decent Syrah,
and a Heated Towel Rack

"The world is a book, and those who do not travel read only one page."

—St. Augustine

"If it looks good in Guatemala, leave it in Guatemala."

—Dame Edna

True Travel Story (You Can't Make These Things Up)

Back in the days of glamorous and glorious transatlantic crossings, a wealthy dowager had traveled with friends (first class, of course) from Europe to New York on one of the legendary ships, like the *Normandie* or *Queen Mary*. As she got off the ship, she announced in a loud and imperious voice, "Oh, it's so good to be back on *terra cotta.*"

First of all, let's be clear. We all, in our heart of hearts, believe that *we* are travelers and all those others are just tourists. "Tourist" is a pejorative whereas "traveler" has everything to do with superiority and a nobler vision and going to Singapore before there were direct flights and when Belize was still British Honduras. Being a "traveler" speaks of "enlightenment" and "discovery" not of sightseeing, souvenir shopping, or packaged tours. It's about taking a "journey" not a "trip." It says that when you come back you will know more about a culture, a civilization, a way of life, *yourself.* And if you just happen to be a "traveler" who stops by the Stanley Market in Hong Kong where you "discover" a great double strand of perfectly matched pure white freshwater pearls for about a quarter of what you'd pay at home, it wouldn't be a terrible thing. Pearls can be enlightening too.

My then-husband and daughters (we fancied ourselves travelers, not tourists) had a mantra that we would recite whenever we saw something on a trip we particularly disdained: a family wearing bright yellow elasticized jogging suits and dirty old sneakers on the plane to France; someone pushing his/her way in front of the crowd to get a better look at the *Mona Lisa*; a bunch of tourists talking really loudly in a small local restaurant; someone rudely demanding directions from a local and then not saying thank you; a middle-aged man or woman wearing nothing but short shorts and a tank top inside a church; someone taking a picture of an adorable child in a foreign country without asking permission first; a "garden lover" picking flowers in the gardens of Giverny; someone saying "Gross!" when the waiter served them the black squid ink risotto they ordered in Venice. "They have as much right to be here as we do," we would recite, in unison at every sighting. We didn't mean it, we didn't believe it, but it did make us feel a little better.

Meanwhile, I, of course, had the child, who on a glorious autumn canoe trip in the White Mountains—three hours into a week-long trip—looked up at the foliage and announced: "I'm sick of trees." Dining in France, this same unnamed child insisted that for her main course she would like an order of pomme frites and plain unbuttered pasta, totally flummoxing even the most unflappable French waiter or waitress.

But whether it's the White Mountains or the Great Wall, the goal of travel is pretty simple: to find the joy in the journey; to adapt to the place where you are, accepting and respecting local customs; to become a more global and worldly person without being snobby about it and praying that the "one of a kind" jade bracelet you buy in Beijing isn't going to be on sale at Banana Republic when you get home. This chapter will help do all of the above. Not only do I now know a lot about getting the most out of a trip, I have learned it all the hard way by getting the *least* out of my own trips. For example: not realizing I needed a passport to go on a cruise to Bermuda (missed the boat); drinking the water when they said *don't* drink the water in Belize (getting dysentary); getting on the line for domestic travel instead of international to Puerto Rico (missed the plane); being so crazy at work that I raced to the wrong airport for my business trip to London (twice). Let's just say, you can take the girl out of suburban Baltimore but . . .

Often, people jump to the conclusion that traveling a lot as a child is what it takes to help you gain the experience and global perspective you need when you are older. This is only partly true, because while travel at a young age *is* illuminating, the single biggest determinant of being at ease anywhere in the world is rooted in the travel DNA we are *born* with. There are timid travelers like me who will happily go anywhere at the drop of a hat but who have to work very hard at not bringing with them all sorts of anxieties and fears. Then there are totally intrepid travelers, like my friend Deborah.

While Deborah is happy in a yurt or a youth hostel where twelve people share an unheated bathroom, I seem to assimilate most quickly in a place with an Ionic hairdryer and European shams and feather duvets and crisp sheets and French doors to a balcony overlooking some body of water and a minibar stocked with jumbo macadamias and a split of champagne. I love staying in places that have "palace" or "regal" in their name, like the Gritti Palace, the Cobacabana Palace, the Rihga Royal. My idea of roughing it is if the hotel doesn't give you conditioner for your hair.

Lest you think I am a total spoiled brat, I have survived llama treks in Maine, camping trips in Yosemite, and spas that only serve wine *once* during the entire week you're there. Frankly, I prefer to think of myself as a "discerning" traveler who is both deeply grateful for hand-milled soap in the bathroom and profoundly moved by the smallest travel experiences: sunset over the Grand Canyon; dusk at Angkor Wat; a gondola ride in Venice.

This is a chapter for me and for Deborah. For the timid and the intrepid. For the neophyte and the experienced. For those who prefer the art at the Prado to those who prefer the art of Prada. But for *all* of us, no matter what our DNA, there are ways to make the trip more memorable, the journey easier, the good times better, the middle seat rarely a possibility.

TRAVEL: IT AIN'T WHAT IT USED TO BE. HOW TO MAKE IT BETTER

The good news is that it is a small world after all, and there are very few places you *can't* get to. Just good luck getting there with even a modicum of comfort or ease if the words *budget* or *coach* figure anywhere in your trip planning. And hope that you're in one of the few places left that doesn't know what a Big Mac is.

Wendy Perrin, who writes the chatty and helpful monthly column "The Perrin Report" for *Condé Nast Traveler* magazine, says, "Fifteen years ago, you could utter certain magic words to an airline agent or a hotel clerk and a first-class seat or a room with a view would materialize before your very eyes." Ms. Perrin laments that "in this era of airline stinginess and undertrained staffs, it's tougher to get more than you paid for; you're lucky if you get what you're due in the first place." Ms. Perrin adds that "every day we receive complaints from readers who are outraged that there was no caviar or filet mignon on their budget cruise."

It can be easier if you use a travel agent, especially if your trip involves more than one airline, lots of connections, a few different countries, and a complicated itinerary. Or you have a business meeting halfway around the world that you *can't* miss. Or if you are going to a number of countries and the planning is complicated. Or, if on your own, you wouldn't begin to know how to plan a great safari or find the best cooking school in Provence.

Access to an airplane lounge can be an invaluable perk on a long trip or when you have an endless layover or when the airport is as crowded as a city bus terminal. Relax, use the internet, have a drink, even take a shower or get your hair cut in some of the spiffiest ones. Skytrax Research "2005 Best Airline Lounges Survey" (1.4 million flyers contributed) ranked international lounges. Check it out at www.airlinequality.com or www.skytraxsurveys.com.

You don't have to fly first or business to get access to a lounge. You can join a program like www.prioritypass.com or www .loungepass.com and pay a fee per visit.

SPEAK UP

Flight attendants may not have time to fully assess a situation and provide fair and wise counsel. That's if you even *see* one on your flight. A few years ago, Phoebe was flying coach to California on a plane that had very little legroom. The man in front of her put his seat all the way back, practically in her lap as soon as the plane took off. Phoebe, to get any space at all, put her seat back too. So it was kind of a domino effect. When the harried flight attendant was hitting into people with her cart—I mean serving soft drinks and snacks—the guy behind Phoebe complained and asked the attendant to make Phoebe put her seat up. Which Phoebe did. The problem was that the flight attendant didn't ask the guy *in front* of Phoebe to do the same thing. So Phoebe couldn't even open her tray table. Erik Torkells, editor in chief of *Budget Travel* magazine hearing this story, says, "Speak up. Say something to the flight attendant. Even if you're young; even if you're shy; even if the flight attendants are really busy."

If I have learned one thing from my travel magazine subscriptions it's *get it in writing*. Your rental car has a couple of pre-dents and dings—get it in writing. You have a confirmed reservation at the inn? Get it in writing. The rug dealer swears it's an antique? Get it in writing.

There's a great book, *Traveller's Rights: Your Legal Guide to Fair Treatment and Full Value,* by Alexander Anolik and John K. Hawks (Sphynx Publishing). Mr. Hawks is executive director of the nonprofit Consumer Travel Rights Center. It all comes down to "persistence and documentation," says Mr. Hawks in a book that really shows you your traveler's Miranda rights.

Tips on complaining when you didn't get what you asked for, from *Condé Nast Traveler* Consumer News Editor Wendy Perrin: "With a solution in mind, just politely and firmly say 'That's unacceptable.' Ask to speak to a manager." She adds, "At hotel front desks, as a general rule never accept a no from someone who isn't empowered to give you a yes in the first place."

PERKS, UPGRADES, FREQUENT FLYER PRIVILEGES

Remember when people told you that you had a shot at getting upgraded if you dressed nicely, asked politely, checked in at the first class counter, told the airline employee that you would really appreciate a little extra legroom? Forget it. Those days ended with the Pan Am Clipper. Upgrades these days *maybe* if you use your miles *and* pay.

If you want perks or more than a bag of stale mini-pretzels, fly business class or first class. Travel with a luxury group like Lindblad Travel or Butterfield & Robinson. Stay at a Relais & Château hotel.

Even being a frequent flyer doesn't mean what it used to. Lots of airlines are doubling and tripling the miles you need to get a free trip. There are so many blackout dates when you can't fly. Some miles expire. Only gold and platinum members are really treated well. And it's not getting better. Gloria Greenstein, a well-traveled travel consultant at Altour Travel, points out that "the whole program has changed. Airlines were supposed to use it as a way to reward their loyal customers. Now with people getting miles from credit cards and planes being full much of the time, it's a business, not a loyalty program."

I will say that Virgin still seems to care. About six months ago, I was flying back from London in business class (thank God for corporate travel) and I noticed that the usually spotless bathroom had wet paper towels next to the sink and someone had spilled hand lotion onto the floor. The flight attendants spent a lot of this uncrowded flight chitchatting in the back and never bothered to straighten up the bathroom. So I emailed the airline and suggested that perhaps they could have made a little effort, especially since Virgin prides itself (rightly) on their attention to detail. One day later they wrote back, thanked me for my letter, and added 10,000 frequent flyer miles to my account. (Do *not* do this or they will know you read this book.)

The airlines might not be giving anything away, but *you* can. *Condé Nast Traveler* says that you can buy airline gift certificates. "The standard minimum for airline gift certificates is $25; most must be used within a year, and some are transferable; if the recipient is a member of a frequent flyer program, you may be able to deposit miles directly into his or her account for about two cents a mile. They suggest www.miles4sale as a good site for purchasing airline miles or www.cruise411.com for contributing toward a cruise. For one-stop shopping, try www.frequentflyer.com. This site profiles airline, hotel, and charge-card reward programs.

How to Get a Free Drink on JetBlue.

That's right, notoriously thrifty JetBlue *insisted* that I accept a glass of Chardonnay on a flight to California last August. You can get one too. Just call my daughter Phoebe and her boyfriend Jake and volunteer to take their two cats across the country. You will have to bring along with you Phoebe's best friend Lindsay, but I'm sure she's game and the scratches on her leg have probably faded by now. To make a long story short, Benjamin and Chloe (known on the manifest as "Cat #1 and Cat #2") were supposed to travel from New York to Oakland, California, in regulation-sized carrying cases that fit under the seat of any airline (they didn't fit JetBlue). They were supposed to take a drug with their preflight food so they would sleep (they wouldn't). The security guy insisted we take these obviously criminal-looking cats *out of their boxes* so they could see if they were packing pistols in their crates. (After Lindsay, who is young and gorgeous, *begged* the security guys not to, we didn't.) When it became clear the cases would *not* fit under the seats, we had to transfer (with the help of two passengers and one sumo-sized flight attendant) hysterical Cat #1 and uncontrollable Cat #2 to smaller JetBlue cardboard boxes. Other passengers were glaring at us. During the flight one cat was wide awake and mewing. The other did swallow some of her little pill—then her eyes rolled back in her head and Lindsay and I both thought she was dead. That's when I got the free drink, which I really appreciated considering that we still had to transfer the cats *back* to their original boxes when we landed. Did I tell you that the guy in the middle seat (we *begged* them not to put someone in the middle seat) was allergic to cats? Much seat changing ensued. The moral, in Dr. Seussian terms: "If you want a free drink when you fly on JetBlue, just make sure you fly with Cat #1 and Cat #2."

PACKING/UNPACKING/REPACKING

- Patricia Volk, novelist and journalist, has a great tip for packing and shopping abroad: "When I travel, I bring all the clothes I hate the most. I wear them once or twice on my trip, then I leave them behind at each hotel when I check out. That way, my suitcase gets lighter, I get rid of clothes I didn't like to begin with, and I have room (and license) to buy new stuff to replace the old." She adds, "While I'm divesting myself, I sing Billie Holiday's 'Travelin' Light.'"

- Marsha Dick and her husband Joey, who belong to the "Carry Your Own Bag" school, had a great test for whether bags were light enough when they went on a family trip. After their two young sons packed their bags, each had to do a practice walk down their driveway and back. If the boys could easily carry their bags without help, they were fine. Otherwise Marsha and Joey had them take stuff out until they could manage.

- Then there is my friend Dorothy, who is a bit contrarian: "Travel these days is just as romantic as women who wear sneakers with business suits. Ugh. You go online and get your own reservation; you print out your own e-ticket; you carry your own bags; you wait in line for checking your bag; you wait in line for security; you bring your own food. Maybe just to fight back, her contrarian motto is "F**k it. Pack it." She packs absolutely everything and doesn't think twice about it.

- What to pack from a New York fashion designer: "extra undies; white tank tops. And one outfit per day. I've been traveling for work for seventeen years and I pack very light. No extras. Just a good book and the computer if I have to bring it for work."

- For reasons that have little to do with the ease of carry-ons in the days of no porters, no help, long waits at the baggage claim, et cetera., traveling as lightly as possible is now seen as something *worthy*. It is a badge of your worldliness and hipness. "That's *all* you're bringing?" is one of the highest compliments you can get. Checking your bag is now another sign of a *tourist,* not a traveler.

- Just about (I know this is a sweeping generalization) every cool person I know wears jeans for long transatlantic flights. And if they are well cut, well fitted, I think jeans make perfect sense. They're comfortable, they don't really wrinkle, and worn with say, a great cashmere sweater or beautifully cut jacket, your fashion statement is that you're too cool for school.

HOW TO MAKE THE FLIGHT MORE BEARABLE

- Aside from the teensiest taste of Ambien so you can sleep, just about everyone who flies a lot swears by noise-canceling headphones. "You don't realize," says Erik Torkells of *Budget Travel* magazine, "how annoying the noise in a plane is until you take them off. And it makes the sound of anything you're listening to so much better."

- Do *not* get the middle seat. You can avoid this by booking early. If I'm doing this on the phone, I always say, "Are you *sure* it's not a middle seat?" and hope that they would feel guilty lying to me. Sometimes you can get lucky and get the spacious emergency row seats since on many airlines these aren't given away until the day of the flight. Travel pro Gloria Greenstein says: "If you never want a middle seat or a bad seat—meaning near the lavatory or so far from the plane door that you will be the last to get off and the last in the customs line—use a travel agent." Her logic is that if a travel agent gets you a bad seat you won't go back to them.

- Or you can go to www.seatguru.com and look at seat configurations ahead of time. This popular site gives helpful tips about things like legroom and location, too.

- Bring food with you in case your flight plane is delayed— something with a long shelf life, like almonds and dried apricots, will get you all the way to Japan. Bring food with you on any domestic flight, even ones that promise you "a snack." If you can exist on a tiny piece of processed cheese, an apple, some bland crackers, and stale biscotti for six hours—more power to you. Otherwise, bring enough yummy stuff to keep you full and happy. And a big bottle of water. Steer clear of bringing on fragrant Indian curries or the fish and chips you bought four hours before you got on the plane. One of the best and funniest ways to see what the airlines are serving (if anything) is to go to www.air planemeals.net, which give meal reviews and great photos of what's on the tray. Proving that this really is a global village a little niche website—www.mgnewman.com/narita/ index.html—is one guy's attempt to help anyone with a long layover at the Tokyo Airport in Narita. He suggests short trips, popular bars, hotels where flight crews stay, local karaoke bars.

ON THE PLANE

- From Erik Torkells, "Bulkhead is overrated. You can't put anything at your feet—it all has to go into the overhead. There's not that much more room for your legs. The tray table is weirdly placed."

- Mr. Torkells says his #1 rule is: "Sit on the aisle. At least you have the illusion of freedom."

- From my experience, bulkhead seats are most often given to moms with little babies. Can you say "frequent cryers"?

- Get on first so the overhead over your seat isn't already full with the huge oversized bags you're not supposed to be able to carry on and the flight attendant just gives you that shrug, as if to say, "What do you expect me to do about it?"

- Save your boarding pass in case you don't get your frequent flyer miles put into your account or you have some dispute with the airline later. Or in case someone comes on the plane with a boarding pass for the identical seat! This is always an exciting moment!

AT THE BAGGAGE CAROUSEL
(FUNNY, IT DOESN'T *LOOK* LIKE A CAROUSEL)

- Lost luggage? Something missing from your bag when it arrives? Damaged suitcase? John Hawks, a travel columnist and the founding editor of the *Consumer Reports Travel Letter,* says, "Don't walk away unless you've gotten what you needed from the baggage services agent. The key is to get it in writing what the airline will do and the person's name who took your claim."

- From *Condé Nast Traveler:* "An airline will reimburse you a maximum of $2,800 for bags that are lost, stolen, or damaged; on international flights that drops to about $1,500 per passenger." The magazine adds, "And you must usually file a claim within twenty-four hours."

- In case you see a medium-sized blue bag with a red gingham bikini in it, that would be the bag that vanished into thin air when I was coming back from Club Med in Martinique fifteen years ago. I still picture it going around the world, from place to place.

WHAT SEASONED TRAVELERS KNOW

- Make use of the hotel concierge before you even get there. Start an email relationship to find out about dinner reservations or to get help with tickets to a sold-out show. Then introduce yourself when you check in so you can put a face to a name and say thank-you. The best thank you, of course, is to tip him or her when you leave.

- Travel is broadening. Sometimes in ways you don't want. Even if the hotel doesn't have a gym, you can stay in shape by doing mat exercises in your room. If you don't know good ones, ask a trainer or tear out some from *Fitness* magazine. Bring a few Dyna-Bands with you and you can get some great stretches. Bring your running shoes too, even though they weigh a ton.

- Check www.weather.com before you leave to see the forecast for the week.

- Go online and figure out currency conversion so you don't have to figure it out when you're jet-lagged and have to pay a taxi driver.

- The book, *Hotel Secrets from the Travel Detective,* by Peter Greenberg, gives down-to-earth advice, smart insights, and tips on everything from hotels to restaurants to safety and security from someone who really knows what he is talking about.

- Also by Mr. Greenberg: *The Travel Detective Flight Crew Confidential.* The subtitle says it all: "People Who Fly for a Living Reveal Insider Secrets and Hidden Values in Cities and Airports Around the World."

- Travel Karma: For every time you are kind enough to tell someone which way the highway is or where to wait for the bus or how to get to the botanical garden in *your* country, you will be rewarded by someone doing the equivalent for you in *their* country. It's like a chain letter that works.

- The postcard rule: Devised by two women friends who traveled all over the world together after college and relied more on their instincts than on guidebooks. Immediately upon arriving in a new place they would stop at the nearest newsstand or store and examine all the postcards. If there were only a few—showing the obligatory church and local botanical gardens or featuring some local attraction like the world's largest wooden clog—they would decide on the spot it wouldn't be worth staying for an extended period.

- When in doubt at a restaurant in a foreign country, see what everyone near you is eating that looks good, discretely point to it and then quote from *When Harry Met Sally,* "I'll have what she's having." Or bring along a copy of *Point It* by Dieter Graf. This little godsend has over 1,000 photos of useful items you don't know how to ask for.

- If you walk into the tiny, out-of-the-way restaurant in a foreign country and everyone at every table is speaking English, leave. This happened to me in Venice. Obviously, all of us had someone give us the name of this same "only the locals go there" place.

- If you are a little fanatical about hygiene (my friend Marsha is so germophobic that she opens ladies' room doors with her elbow), you might be interested in www.thebathroom diaries.com. It's a site that tells you how travelers rate facilities near tourist sites around the world.

- Get a quick overview of options for local *anything*: The Lonely Planet books are good, so is the website www.lonely planet.com. Another great choice is the Essential Series. AA World Travel Guides (www.theaa.com). Smart, succinct guides to dozens of cities and countries from a British publisher. Maps, photos, top sites to visit, best restaurants, best way to get from here to there, currency, et cetera—all in one small, literate, easy-to-carry book.

WHAT SEASONED BUSINESS TRAVELERS KNOW

- From Peter Greenberg, travel editor for *The Today Show*: "Don't ever order Eggs Benedict from room service, as eggs with thick sauces don't travel well." I am a firm believer that chilled Chardonnay and Cobb salads are excellent travelers.

- If you're traveling by yourself, never take the hotel room on the ground floor or on the second floor overlooking the parking lot. Don't take the room with a fire escape right outside. Don't take the one where construction is being done outside the room or under it. Try not to take a room that's part of a connecting suite and has a shared door. If there's a concierge floor with a special access key, ask to stay on that floor. (Executive floors also tend to have free drinks and hors d'oeuvres at cocktail time and free coffee in the morning.) If your hotel is in a dicey part of the city, don't take a room with a balcony or terrace. From my experience, the minute you say to a desk clerk, "I don't feel safe in that room" and give the reason, you will be switched.

• The bottle of mineral water on the desk in your hotel room that looks like it's free isn't.

• Problems: Find someone in charge so you can register a complaint, ask that a problem be rectified, or just to praise good service. Peter Greenberg even sends thank-you notes to a concierge, hotel manager, or airline clerk who has come through for him in a pinch. (NB: It is people like Mr. Greenberg who do *not* get the hotel room that faces the brick wall.)

• Book the city hotel with the pool if you love to swim and start the day doing laps. On a cautionary note, from my experience, some of these pools are tiny and creepy and weren't worth the sacrifice of a more expensive room or less convenient location. Try to find out specifics on pool/gym/spa facilities, either from the hotel or from the website. I recently stayed at a premium hotel in Toronto that boasted "a fully equipped gym" that turned out to be two treadmills, three weight machines, and a broken television in the basement next to the boiler room.

• The rule of thumb is to tip the person who cleans your room if you have stayed more than three days.

• *Business Travel: When It's Your Money*, by Ed Perkins. While this is more for, in Mr. Perkins's words, "independent professionals, lawyers, consultants, small business owners," this book has some helpful advice for anyone who wants to be a savvier flyer. Mr. Perkins tells readers how to look for affordable options in an industry where low-cost travel, at least, "is a really, really bad product."

What Women Know

There are many companies and sites just for women's travel, whether it's a spa week, an athletic adventure a shopping trip, an ecological tour, or a spiritual retreat. The website www.journeywoman.com has 45,000 subscribers worldwide and offers up-to-date travel news plus links to hundreds of upcoming trips, just for women. Here's one of my favorites:

Buenos Aires Tango Tour for Women. Tanguera Tours offers a unique ten-day journey into learning tango, living the drama and romance of Buenos Aires's dance halls, fulfilling your dance dreams, and pampering yourself to the max. No prior tango experience or knowledge necessary. Website: www.tangueratours.com

Other women's travel sites include www.gutsywomentravel .com and www.shoparoundtours.com.

TRAVEL TIPS AND ASSORTED WISDOM

- For a long plane trip (California, Hong Kong), bring a *backup* book too in case you hate the first one and then have nothing to read but the in-flight magazine for twelve hours.

- Whether you're checking your luggage or bringing carry-on, pack a small bag with all meds, a toothbrush, comb, and underwear, especially when you are flying internationally. Bring sanitary products even if you aren't expecting your period. Bring an extra T-shirt too in case your luggage is lost or if you just want to create the illusion of freshness when you land. Bring a few extra plastic bags for wet bathing suits, the seashells you've collected, et cetera.

- If you ask a concierge in, say, Paris, for a restaurant recommendation and he says, "Well, there's really only *one* I wouldn't miss if I were you," you know it's owned by his brother-in-law.

- If the local *Time Out* or this year's edition of Fodor's says a place is "undiscovered" and well worth it, you can figure it will be mobbed and the prices will have tripled by the time you get there. And that's if it's still open at all.
- From well-traveled advertising executive Nancy McNally: "The more expensive the hotel, the better you sleep."
- Bring an extra soft duffel or soft backpack to pack in your bag to take home what you buy on your trip.
- Bring small sealable plastic bags with you so your suntan lotion won't leak or explode in your bag. Don't bring *anything* (moisturizer, hand cream) in a glass jar.
- Take the vacation you can't afford and love it.

LOCAL CUSTOMS

- While there is a law now that you can take your unfinished bottle of wine home with you in France, don't ever ask for a doggie bag to take your leftovers home.
- In Mexico, don't eat the guacamole because of the water that washes the tomato and cilantro that go into it.
- You know it's "St. Barth's," not "St. Barts." But does it really make a difference?
- The French and Italians cut everything with forks that we eat with our hands—pizza, panini, sandwiches, chicken wings.
- In Capri most of the really good shops (YSL, Gucci, Prada) close during the day when day-trippers (more frugal sightseers than free-spending fashionistas) come over from Naples. So when in Capri, plan to shop after the last ferry leaves.
- Fodor's advises, "Never order sushi in a landlocked country."
- Of course, the Russians have never heard of Russian dressing. Italians never put a piece of lemon zest in *their* espresso. The French don't call them French fries, and they would probably sue us if they tried what we call "French dressing."

- What not to wear when you're abroad: A savvy traveler says, "Short *anything*!!!! Don't invite a disaster. It's not as accepted elsewhere as it is here. You'll be looked at like a hooker." And I would say it goes without saying but it doesn't seem to these days: no sleeveless diaphanous microminis at the Vatican or in a Muslim country. No jangling bracelets in a place of worship. Dress up for fancy restaurants—find out ahead if they have a dress code. Be sensitive. Be respectful. Use common sense.

WHAT TO WEAR AND WHERE

- "In Capri," notes Nancy McNally, "the baggage boy at the hotel looks chicer than 99 percent of the tourists." Rules of thumb: Do not wear jogging suits; try to find a pair of walking shoes that isn't some version of pink-and-metallic-striped Adidas; avoid (especially in a chic city like Paris or Venice) being in one of those tour groups where you all get free plastic color-tinted ponchos and follow the leader who is waving a large umbrella.

- I am not a big fan of those catalogues selling "travel clothes." They always seem way more sensible than fashionable and flattering. The word *frumpy* comes to mind. And just because something isn't going to wrinkle on a three-week trip doesn't mean it's going to look good on you. There are so many options now of thin, easily washable cottons and nonwrinkling jerseys; year-round cashmeres and washable silks that work in most climates and so many ways you can layer and still maintain some style, that it's not that hard to look pulled together and presentable.

- I'm sorry to have to say this, but in a really nice hotel or restaurant, things like old fraying stained suitcases and terrible clothes equal terrible rooms, uninterested service, and bad tables. One solution: www.flight001.com. Cool travel stuff, high-quality luggage and accessories (not cheap, but they do have great sales). And if you're not staying at the

Ritz, try www.llbean.com and www.landsend.com for handsome hardworking duffels and basic suitcases.

- Your shopping mantra: "Of course I should buy it. When am I ever going to be back in _____?" (Fill in blank.)

- But don't buy things that look great *there* but that you won't (or *shouldn't*) wear at home. (Or if you *do,* you'll feel like a large version of those costume dolls from around the world.) Dirndl-skirted folkloric dresses from Eastern Europe; voluminous velvet Rembrandt shawls from Holland; cowboy shirts and chunky turquoise jewelry from Arizona, the pointy Alladin slides that *everyone* was wearing in Bangkok. You never want to walk into a room and have someone say, "Oh, you've just been to _____!"

- If it's a serious purchase, make sure that whatever you are buying is authentic and indigenous and okay to take out of the country (you can't take anything with a Buddha likeness out of Cambodia, for example) and be sure you're not getting something you could get more easily and for less online: espadrillesetc.com in Spain is a good example.

- Bring home something local so you'll have something tangible to remember your trip by. On the other hand, if *all* you remember about the trip *is* the shopping, that's not good. Trust me, I know. So when you go to the museum or duomo, don't think "gift shop" until afterward.

- The real problem with foreign shopping is that what you buy usually looks even *better* once you get it home. It's the "Why Didn't I Buy More" problem. So if you are buying a cute red plastic cherry pin, a hand-crocheted bracelet for a friend, a hand-carved coconut serving spoon, buy two. Or three. That way you can have one for yourself without being wracked with guilt for keeping it or wracked with remorse for giving it to a friend.

- Most airport gourmet shops in Europe will be able to vacuum seal any cheese you buy there, so it's legal to take it home with you. Cheeses sealed in wax (Harrods in

Heathrow has these) are also okay. Most gourmet cheese stores or upscale markets in Europe or Scandinavia either have vacuum-sealed cheeses or will seal them for you. Goat cheeses, Gouda, all hard cheeses travel well. Don't risk alienating your entire plane with a ripe Gorgonzola.

- From *Condé Nast Traveler*'s Insider Secrets: "If you can't carry it home, don't buy it." They add, "While there are laws in place to protect you from consumer fraud in the United States, you have no legal recourse with unscrupulous merchants abroad."

- There are all sorts of things that different countries seem to claim as being exclusive to their artists and artisans. I have seen batik (toilet kits, duffels), for example, everywhere from Mexico to Malaysia to Rio. Do people make batik in *all* these places? Same with glass rings, wooden salad bowls, thin hammered silver bracelets, pleated tie-dyed cotton scarves. And the quality isn't at all what you would expect from something lovingly crafted. In fact, Anika Chapin notes, "The most well known are the most likely to have been coopted into cheesy tourist schlock." When her sister Zoe traveled to the Aran Isles, islands renowned for their knitwear, most of the sweaters and scarves were mass produced in Japan and imported. Globalization at the bazaar. Bizarre.

- If you think you're going to buy something much more expensive than you normally would (say, gold earrings in Rio or a Chanel bag in Paris), call your credit card company before you leave home and alert them. Otherwise they're likely to think someone has stolen your card and deny the transaction. That's what happened to my friend Barbara who had one too many glasses of sangria and said yes to the chunky emerald ring in the store across the street from the restaurant.

Not Lost in Translation: How to Ask Your Most Important Global Shopping Questions

1. I'm just looking. Thank you.

Hebrew: *Ahnee rahk meestahkelet. Todah.*

Italian: *Vorrei solo dare un'occhiata, grazie.*

Chinese: *Xie xie, wo yao kan kan.*

French: *Je jète une oeil seulement. Merci.*

Spanish: *No, gracias. Solamente estoy mirando.*

2. Is it okay if I just look? Thank you.

Hebrew: *Ah-eem zeh beseder sheh ahnee rahk meestahkelet? Todah.*

Italian: *Posso dare un'occhiata? Grazie.*

Chinese: *Wo ke yi kan kan ma? Xie xie.*

French: *Ça ne vous gène pas si je regarde seulement? Merci.*

Spanish: *Nada más quiero revisar. ¿Está bien?*

3. Could you tell me how much that is in dollars?

Hebrew: *Camah zeh oleh beh dohlahreem?*

Italian: *Mi può dire quanto viene questo in dollari?*

Chinese: *Yao duo shao mei jin?*

French: *Ça fait combien en dollars?*

Spanish: *¿Por favor, me puede decir cuanto vale en dólares?*

4. Is there a sale rack?

Hebrew: *Yesh leh-hem sale?*

Italian: *Ci sono articoli in saldo?*

Chinese: *Jian jia huo you ma?*

French: *Vous avez des vêtements en soldes?*

Spanish: *¿Tiene una percha con ropa en especial?*

5. Is that price firm? Can you do any better?

Hebrew: *Ah-eem efshar leh-horeed bah meeheer?*

Italian: *Il prezzo è fisso? O si può fare un po' di sconto?*

Chinese: *Zhe shi ding jia? Ke yi jian jia ma*

French: *Est-ce que c'est votre dernier prix? Pourriez-vous faire mieux?*

Spanish: *¿Ese es el mejor precio que puede dar, o me puede dar más rebaja?*

6. Do I look fat in this: bikini, dirndl, pareo, spandex catsuit?

Hebrew: *Ah-eem ahnee neeret shmenah bezeh? Ah-eem ahnee neeret shmenah bezeh bikini hazeh?* (You can substitute dirndl, pareo, and spandex catsuit where the word *bikini* is.) The first sentence here is just the question: "Do I look fat in this?" The next question is Do I look fat in this "X."

Italian: *Come mi questa gonna, questo pareo, questa tuta? Sembro grassa?*

Chinese: *Wo kan tai pang ma?: bikini——*

French: *Est-ce que cela me grossit: maillot de bain, dirndl, paréo, combinaison spandex?*

Spanish: *¿Me veo gorda con este bikini? Falda? Pareo? Enter-izo?*

7. This is cut very small. Do you have anything in my size?

Hebrew: *Zeh catahn (gadohl). Yesh mashu bah meedah shelee?* (*Gadol* means "large.")

Italian: *Questa taglia è troppo piccola, c'è una taglia più grande?*

Chinese: *Zhe jian tai xiao liao. Ni you wo di che cun ma?*

French: *C'est trop juste. Est-ce que vous avez quelque chose à ma taille?*

Spanish: *Este es me queda pequeño. ¿Tiene algo en mi talla?*

8. Is this for a child?

Hebrew: *Ah-eem zeh behshveel yeladeem?*

Italian: *Questo è per una bambina?*

Chinese: *Zhe shi wei xiao hai zi di?*

French: *C'est pour un enfant?*

Spanish: ¿Esto es para niños?

9. I can't get it over my head to take it off.

Hebrew: *Ahnee lo yeh-hola la-ahveer etzeh meh-ahl ha-rosh.*

Italian: *Questo non mi passa la testa, non riesco a toglierlo.*

Chinese: *Wo di tou la bu chu lai.*

French: *Je ne peut pas le passer par la tête.*

Spanish: *No puedo sacarlo por mi cabeza.*

10. Do you speak English?

Hebrew: *Aht meedaberet eevreet?*

Italian: *Parla inglese?*

Chinese: *Ni hui shui ying wen ma?*

French: *Parlez-vous anglais?*

Spanish: ¿Habla inglés?

11. Why didn't you tell me you spoke English?

Hebrew: *Lahmah lo ahmart lee sheh aht meedahberet eevreet?*

Italian: *Perché non mi ha detto che parla l'inglese?*

Chinese: *Ni wei she me bu gao su wo, ni hui shui ying wen?*

French: *Pourquoi vous ne m'avez pas dit que vous parliez anglais?*

Spanish: ¿Porque no me dijo que usted habla inglés?

12. Can you ship it?

Hebrew: *Yohleem leeshloah etzeh?*

Italian: *Si può spedirmelo?*

Chinese: *Ni ke yi yun ma?*

French: *Pourriez-vous l'expédier?*

Spanish: *¿Usted melo enviar a mi casa?*

13. Can I bring this through customs?

Hebrew: *Ahnee yechola la-ahveer etzeh bah-mehes?*

Italian: *Me fanno passare per la dogana con questa?*

Chinese: *Wo ke yi dai chu hai guan ma?*

French: *Est-ce que je peut le passer à la douane?*

Spanish: *¿Voy a poder pasarlo por aduana?*

14. Are you sure this is angora, not cat fur?

Hebrew: *Ah-eem zeh ahmeetee veh lo heekuwee?* (The literal translation here is: "Is it real or is it fake?" They don't even sell angora or cat fur in Israel so there is no specific Hebrew word for either, but just in case.)

Italian: *Lei è sicura che è lana d'angora vera, non pelo di gatto?*

Chinese: *Zhe shi zhen di angora yang mao? Bu shi mao mao?*

French: *Vous êtes sûr que c'est de l'angora et non pas du chat?*

Spanish: *¿Está seguro que esto es lana de angora y no piel de gato?*

15. What does "100 percent pure cashmere" mean?

Hebrew: *Mah hamuvahn shel meh-ah ahooz cajmeer?* (Literal translation: "What is meant by 100 percent cajmeer?" Essentially you have to fill in the word in question at the end of the sentence.)

Italian: *Che vuol dire cento per cento cachemire?*

Chinese: *Yi bai fen cashmere shi she me yi si?*

French: *Que signifie "100 pour cent pure cachemire"?*

Spanish: *¿Me puede decir qué significa cien porciento cachemira pura?*

16. Is it old?

Hebrew: *Zeh yahshahn?*

Italian: *È antico?*

Chinese: *Zhe shi lao huo ma?*

French: *Est-ce que c'est vieux?*

Spanish: *¿Es viejo?*

17. Is it real?

Hebrew: *Zeh ahmeetee?*

Italian: *È autentica?*

Chinese: *Zhe shi zhen di ma?*

French: *Est-ce que c'est authentique?*

Spanish: *¿Es real?*

18. Is it a relic? Authentic? Rare? An antique? A reproduction? One of a kind? Handcrafted? Gold? Old?

Hebrew: *Aheem zeh ahmeetee* (authentic)? *Meh-yu-hahd* (special/rare)? *Ahteek* (antique)? *Heekuwee* (a copy)? *Ehad beh minoh* (one in a million)? *Ahvodaht yahd* (handcrafted)? *Zahav* (gold)? *Yahshahn* (old)?

In Hebrew, relic = antique, and rare could equal one-of-a-kind.

Italian: *È una reliquia? Autentico? Raro? Un oggetto di antiquariato? Una reproduzione? Unica? Fatto a mano? D'oro? Vecchio?*

Chinese: *Zhe shi yi wu ma? Zhen di? Xi shao di? Shi gu dong* *ma? Shi fu zhi di ma? Zhi you yi ge? Shou gong zuo di? Jin zi? Lao di?*

French: *Est-ce que c'est authentique? Rare? Une antiquité? Une reproduction? Une pièce unique? De l'artisanat? En or? Ancien?*

Spanish: *¿Es auténtico? ¿Poco común? ¿Es antigüedad? ¿Es una reproducción? ¿Unico? ¿Es hecho a mano? ¿Es hecho en oro? ¿Es viejo?*

19. Is it legal to take it out of the country?

Hebrew: *Ah-eem zeh hukee lehotzee etzeh meh Israel?*

Italian: *Si può legalmente portarlo fuori del paese?*

Chinese: *Ke yi dai chu guo? Bu fan fa?*

French: *Est-ce qu'on peut le sortir légalement du pays?*

Spanish: *¿Se puede sacar del país legalmente?*

20. Where was it made? A factory? By master craftsmen? By blind nuns or entrepreneurial monks? By natives? By locals? By a deranged but brilliant outsider artist? By an indigenous tribe?

Hebrew: *Efoh ahsuh etzeh* (Where did they make this)? *Beh Bet-haroshet* (in a factory)? *Mee ha-Ohmahn* (by master-craftsmen)?

Italian: *Dov'è stato fabbricato? In fabbrica? Da artigiani? Da suore cieche monaci imprenditoriali? Da gente indigena? Da gente della zona? Da un artista estraneo pazzo ma brillante? Da una tribù indigeni?*

Chinese: *Na li zuo di? Gong chang? Gao ji gong jiang? Ben di ren?* (Cannot distinguish between a native and a local person.) (Chinese would not understand "deranged but brilliant outsider artist." The humor will be totally lost on them.) *Shao shu min tsu?*

French: *Où est-ce que c'etait fait? Dans une usine? Par un arti-*

san? Par des bonnes sœurs aveugles ou des moines entrepreneurs? Des indigènes? Des locaux? Par un artiste handicappé mais brillant? Par une tribu indigène?

Spanish: ¿En dónde fue fabricado? ¿Una fábrica? ¿Es en taller de artesanía? ¿Por monjas ciegas o los monjes trabajadores? ¿Por indígenas? ¿Por un artista extranjero que es excéntrico pero increíble?

21. Why does it say what looks like "Made in Poland"? (This question obviously is less compelling if you are shopping in Poland.)

Hebrew: *Lahmah zeh ohmer mashu cmoh "Ahsu-ee beh Polaniah"?*

Italian: *Perché sembra di esserci scritto "Prodotto in Polonia"?*

Chinese: *Zhe hao xiang shui shi Poland zuo di. Shi ma?*

French: *Pourquoi est-ce qu'il y a une étiquette "Fabriqué en Pologne"?*

Spanish: *¿Porque dice que fue "Hecho en Polania"?*

SOME GREAT STORES AND MARKETS AROUND THE WORLD

Amsterdam: Pauw—a store crammed with everything you want and feel you *need*. A great selection of casual, contemporary clothes and shoes, mostly from European designers. Some wonderful up-and-coming Belgian and Dutch designers make it more fun.

Paris: Colette.

London: Willma, 339 Portobello Road. Jemima French, codesigner of FrostFrench from English *Vogue*: "Willma has the cutest and most-wanted accessories—it has beautiful jewelry by the Indian designer Ashish, as well as bags and scarves." Paul & Joe: Small boutiques with everything you want desperately—witty, fresh, delicious separates that feel very one of a kind. Lingerie and accessories too. Expensive to begin with, and killer with a weak U.S. dollar. But a girl can dream. Odie & Amanda: a small shop in the Oxo Tower. Using everything from Balinese cotton to Liberty prints, Australian designer Odie creates clothes that are feminine and fresh; one of a kind. They've been written up in English *Vogue*. Asked for his shopping recommendations, Odie says Selfridges and H&M and all the chic shops in Notting Hill. As for vintage, he recommends Portobello "on Friday, not Saturday," which is when all that's left is "market tat." Friday morning, he says, is when you'll see all the big designers—from Stella McCartney to Paul Smith—sifting through the stuff.

Dublin: Avoca, a sprawling, beautifully designed store. This four-story, family-run emporium has everything from Irish blankets to designer dresses to a popular cafe.

New York: For big stores, Barneys and Bergdorf's. For small, it's endless: you could spend hours in Tribeca and Nolita and the Lower East Side striking gold. For casual and cool and current, there's Calypso, Scoop, Intermix, Mayle, Kirna Zabête. For home furnishings two great choices are Moss and John Derian.

Shanghai: Xintiandi, a luxury shopping and dining complex; a wholesale silk market called Dong Jia Du; Coolyah Antique Furniture.

THERE ARE LITTLE TREASURES THAT WILL HELP YOU DISCOVER LITTLE TREASURES

- *The Antique & Flea Markets of Italy,* by Marina Seveso (The Little Bookroom). A small, selective guide from a seasoned shopper.

- *City Secrets: Rome,* by Robert Kahn, series editor (The Little Bookroom). This isn't a guidebook per se, rather a well-rounded compilation of personal favorites (arts, culture, and food figure prominently) in Rome along with insights and observations, written by some of America's most distinguished artists, writers, archaeologists, and historians. A portion of the proceeds from the sale of this charming guide goes to the American Academy in Rome. Others in this series include: City Secrets guides to *Florence, Venice and the Towns of Italy, London, New York City.* Additionally, there's *The Historic Shops and Restaurants of New York.*

THIRTEEN

*Happily (Relatively Speaking, of Course)
Ever After*

From Ruth Friendly, an accomplished friend who is in her eighties: "The biggest luxury is time. You need to figure out how to spend it wisely."

From a down-to-earth psychotherapist: "Forgive yourself every day."

Mantra from a woman who can live with what she *can't* change: "It is what it is."

From my friend Grace Lee, who knows how to put the right spin on it: "There's always someone who's having a worse hair day, doing worse at work, having a worse time on vacation, seeing a worse movie, giving a worse dinner party."

From Stephen Sondheim: "Even Cream of Wheat has lumps."

"Measure twice. Cut once."

Opera singer Marilyn Horne: "There is the small time, the medium time, and the big time. This is the big time. 'Sing out, Louise!' "

AND FINALLY

If—after all the advice, wisdom, encouragement, and completely humiliating stories mostly of my own that I've managed to cram into this book—you still have some unanswered questions or nagging fears, you shouldn't worry. Or actually, you *should* worry. Because we are all evolving. And because even the richest, fullest, most fabulous life isn't entirely anxiety-free, trouble-free, glitch-free, or worry-free.

We are complex women leading complex lives. Sometimes life is confusing. Sometimes we confuse ourselves. A woman recently wrote in to *Newsweek* in response to an article about personality: "I could never decide if I was an extroverted introvert or an introverted extrovert, an optimistic pessimist or a pessimistic optimist." Welcome to my world.

We all want shoes we can't walk in, men we can't have, the hair we weren't born with, sex without remorse, chocolate without calories, flat stomachs without crunches. But perhaps you will be reassured to know that many of these wishes and worries are ones that, at some point in our lives, we can all relate to or even share. Look, I'm sharing mine:

1. My shrink will die before I do.
2. The Botox will freeze my face permanently.
3. The fruit will rot; the milk will sour; the creamed corn will expire; I'll take the 5-milligram sleeping pill when I wake up instead of the identical-looking calcium pill.
4. I will get older and older with every birthday and Tina Turner will still always be sixty.
5. My adult child will take me to the dog track and leave me there.
6. I will never understand what "second cousin, once removed" means.
7. The avocados will ripen three days before I need to make the guacamole for the party or two days *after* I need to make the guacamole for the party . . . .
8. I'll never know who General Tso is and why a military leader knows so much about making chicken.
9. For my whole life, Pluto was a planet. Then one day it got demoted to "an icy body." How can this happen?
10. I will swim off the edge of the infinity pool.

And, at some point, we all experience the "what was I *thinking*?" kind of thinking that wakes you up around 3:00 a.m. so you can ruminate on your unfortunate choices and decisions. But look at it this way: Isn't it really how *you* choose to look at it? Take it from actress Tallulah Bankhead: "If I had my life to live over again, I'd make the same mistakes, only sooner."

ACKNOWLEDGMENTS

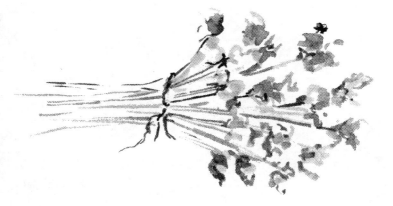

Sydny Miner. Major editor, counsel and friend.

Nina Collins. An agent who's got it all and gives generously.

Anika Chapin. Savvy, sane, sensational since Day One.

Barbara Harrison. #1 in my book.

Matthew Elblonk. How do you say "You're the best" in any language?

With a little help from my friends. Thanks to: Sarah Hochman, Kathryn Letson, Liz Gross Strianese, Pauline Rueda, Tomek Koszylko, Robert Searles, Marylin Silverman, Marsha Dick, Grace Lee, Antonia Green, Nancy Stephens, Phyllis Cohen, Laura Menard, Ray Menard, Molly Friedrich, Fran Sheff Mauer, Elaine McCormick, Dorothy Kalins, Roger Sherman, Marjorie Kalins, Sandrine Lago, Doreen Fox, Dominique Bigar Khan, Mark Finley, Bobbi Schlesinger, Carol Helms, Caroline Schaefer, Miranda Morrison, Mary Ann Restivo, Christiane Celle, Paula Faulk, Catia Chapin, Zoe Chapin, Joanna Chapin, Ruth Friendly, Annette Mark, Patti Goberman, Nancy Jean McNamara, Jane Rosenthal, Dr. Marsha Gordon, Alexis Johnson, Diane Reverand, Patty Thomson, Dr. Jeri Kronen, Gloria Greenstein, Katrina Borgstrom, Lindsay Cain, Abigail Connell, Patrick Melville, Carrie Butterworth, Vernon Mahabal, Jenny Feldman, Lindsay Carleton, Erik Torkells, Debra Braff, Paula Lambert, Scott Pastor, Dr. Jana Klauer, Jean Volpe, Ammi Simon, Patty Volk, Heidi Johnston, Don Florence, Terry Hall, Dr. Harriet Blumencranz, Heather Willensky, Rosalie McCabe Jamrosz, Dr. Steven Gruenstein, Katherine Wagner, Lucinda Williams, Donna Warner, Lida Burpee.

Printed in the United States
By Bookmasters